How To HELP YOUR PASTOR SUCCEED

Moving from the Multitude to the Inner Circle

DAVE WILLIAMS

HOW TO HELP YOUR PASTOR SUCCEED

Moving from the Multitude to the Inner Circle

Unless otherwise noted, Scripture quotations are taken from the King James Version of the Bible.

Scripture quotations marked (Message) are taken from THE MESSAGE. Copyright © 1993, 1994, 1995, 1996, 2000, 2001, 2002. Used by permission of NavPress Publishing Group.

Scripture quotations marked (TLB) are taken for the *Living Bible*. Copyright © 1976. Used by permission of Tyndale House Publishers, Inc. Wheaton, IL 60189

Copyright © 2005 by Dr. David R. Williams

ISBN 0-938020-73-0

First Printing 2005

Cover By: Robison Gamble Creative

Published by

DECAPOLIS
PUBLISHING

Printed in the United States of America

BOOKS BY DAVE WILLIAMS

OTHER BOOKS BY DAVE WILLIAMS

CONTENTS

I*f your pastor is doing his job right, his vision will be shared by the entire church.*

FIRST THOUGHTS

What is your pastor's vision? What are your goals as a church? How are you helping to meet those goals?

This book is for people who want their pastor and their church to succeed. It is for people who share their pastor's vision and want to do all they can to make it come to pass.

A pastor's vision, springing from the heart of God, is the guiding force of a church. If your pastor is doing his job right, his vision will be shared by the entire church. There will be unity. You will have no problem getting behind his strategies for reaching toward the God-given vision.

But even when a pastor has a strong vision, there are many people who do not know how to help him carry it out. Sometimes they become busybodies; their attitudes grow sour because they feel they are not accomplishing as much as they could if their energies were channeled in the right way; or they feel their spiritual or ministry gifts are stifled. They feel frustrated. Sometimes well-meaning people neglect the basic things that would help their pastor the most. They do not understand, from a pastor's perspective, how to advance a church's purpose and vision.

I have been a pastor for more than 25 years and have seen countless ideas that work and countless ideas that do not work in equipping people to help their pastor succeed. Over the years, I have whittled the good concepts down to a select few that I believe are critical for any church to succeed. Those principles are spelled out in this book.

This book is intended to guide you in helping your pastor succeed. We will talk about:

1. *Moving from the multitude to the inner circle.*

2. *Making excuses to get to church instead of making excuses for staying away from church.*

3. *Expecting great things from God.*

4. *Enforcing Christ's victory over the devil.*

5. *Developing a happy, successful home life.*

6. *Echoing the pastor's vision.*

Why is this book important? Because there is a God-given urgency these days to fulfill our destiny as a church. Maybe you feel it. I know I do.

Pastors – everywhere – are in pain. More than anything else they need love, encouragement, and prayer support of the people they serve.

Pastoral service is harder now than ever before.

Time is running out for your church and mine to complete our God-given mandate. The sands of time are falling. Darkness is painted against the sky. Antichrist forces are rising up all around, and soon the world will spiral down into her most severe hour of agony. We must labor together with God's anointed pastors while it is still day.

This simple, straightforward book will help you sharpen your efforts to help your pastor, your church, and the Kingdom of God succeed.

Dave Williams

Lansing, Michigan

Note: Throughout this book I refer to the pastor as "he," because 95% of all pastors are men. This is not to devalue the place of those precious, hard-working women pastors. Please read "he" as being generic and not gender specific.

God wants you to be part
of a winning team
by working together.

CHAPTER

FROM MULTITUDE TO INNER CIRCLE

Think about your church for a moment. If every member were just like you, what kind of church would it be? What kind of place would it be if everyone:

- Gave like you do?
- Prayed for the church like you do?
- Worked for the church like you do?
- Spoke about the church like you do?

Would you want to attend that church?

God made us all unique and special. No two people in any church are just alike, but when it comes to how people relate to their pastor and church, I have noticed they fall into three major categories. Not surprisingly, it was the same in Jesus' day. Now, I realize there are subcategories under each of these major categories, which I expound on in another series. But for the sake of simplicity and clarity, I'll highlight only the three major categories of church goers: (1) the multitude, (2) the provisional disciples, (3) the inner circle.

THE MULTITUDE

These people came to hear Jesus, drawn by their wonder, curiosity, word of mouth, or by their desire to be healed or delivered. Luke 6:17-19 describes them this way:

> And he came down with them, and stood in the plain, and the company of his disciples, and a great multitude of people out of all Judaea and Jerusalem, and from the sea coast of Tyre and Sidon, which came to hear him, and to be healed of their diseases; And they that were vexed with unclean spirits: and they were healed. And the whole multitude sought to touch him: for there went virtue out of him, and healed *them* all.

The New International Version calls them the "large crowd." The King James Version calls them "a great multitude."

Every church has a multitude circle. They usually make up the highest number of people in the congregation. There is an old saying that 20 percent of the people do 80 percent of the work, and that is far too often the case in many churches.

The multitude are those who enjoy the benefits of a church without carrying their share of the responsibilities. They make no long-term commitment. They often try to remain anonymous, avoid recognition, even avoid eye contact, so when they leave, no one will miss them. They are easily drawn away from the church if some other church seems more attractive or if they simply want to spend more time at the lake. They enjoy the preaching and may even weep under the conviction or touch of the Holy Spirit. They enjoy the music, the choir, the upbeat choruses, and the good feeling they get from being in a worship service.

The multitude are those who enjoy the benefits without carrying their share of the responsibilities.

But the multitude cannot be counted on to move the church forward.

Jesus was very gracious toward the multitude. He healed them, cast demons out of them, taught them, fed them, even brought their dead back to life. But He also held them at arm's length. John wrote:

> But Jesus did not commit himself unto them, because he knew all *men.*
>
> —John 2:24

Jesus told the disciples:

> He answered and said unto them, Because it is given unto you to know the mysteries of the kingdom of heaven, but to them it is not given.
>
> —Matthew 13:11

When you remain in the multitude you retain the freedom to come and go without being accountable. In Jesus' day, the multitude would disappear at sundown and reappear at sun up, while the disciples stayed with Jesus. The multitude had comfort but not closeness. They did not feel compelled to give up their particular lifestyle to follow the Son of God.

Sometimes I'll hear statements like this: "I've been going to this church for six years, and I've never met the pastor." My answer is, "You've remained in the multitude; you've never become involved; you've never found time to take one of the pastor's classes or volunteer to help in some way." You choose to step into a more intimate circle. Nobody can do it for you.

Provisional disciples can plug in very quickly, but their roots are shallow, and soon something pulls them away.

But if you stay in the crowd, you lose much more than you retain: deep friendships that can only be forged by serving side-by-side with other believers and spiritual maturity, which can only be gained by pressing in and becoming a functioning member of the body of Christ. The multitude is a good entry point or waiting area for people just coming into the church or for those who have been wounded somehow, but it is not meant to be a permanent dwelling place.

PROVISIONAL DISCIPLES

The second circle of Jesus' followers were the provisional disciples. I call them that because they were not entirely committed, and they attached provisions to their loyalty. There were probably hundreds of those who trailed along behind Him as Jesus went from town to town, who gave the impression of being every bit as dedicated as those in the inner circle. They made public declarations in support of Him. They stayed with Him longer than the multitude. The Bible even says that Jesus loved a man who turned out to be a provisional disciple (the rich young ruler who sadly turned away).

But something keeps provisional disciples from moving completely into the inner circle. We see a quick succession of provisional disciples in Luke 9:57-62:

> And it came to pass, that, as they went in the way, a certain *man* said unto him, Lord, I will follow thee whithersoever thou goest. And Jesus said unto him, Foxes have holes, and birds of the air *have* nests; but the Son of man hath not where to lay *his* head.
>
> And he said unto another, Follow me. But he said, Lord, suffer me first to go and bury my father. Jesus said unto him, Let the dead bury their dead: but go thou and preach the kingdom of God.
>
> And another also said, Lord, I will follow thee; but let me first go bid them farewell, which are at home at my house. And Jesus said unto him, No man, having put his hand to the plough, and looking back, is fit for the kingdom of God.

Each of these three men surfaced for a brief moment in the Gospels then disappeared forever from the divine record. They did not have staying power, despite their pledge of loyalty. When the time came to put up or shut up, they made excuses:

"Let me bury my father."

"Let me say good-bye to my family."

Jesus read the heart of the first man who approached Him

and knew that his propensity for comfort would ultimately draw him away.

Have you known a provisional disciple? Someone who burst onto the scene with enthusiasm and promise then abruptly disappeared?

Provisional disciples can "plug in" very quickly. Suddenly they are planning Sunday school functions, supplying donuts and coffee on Sunday morning, and talking about their love of the church. But their roots are shallow, and soon something pulls them away.

Churches are full of provisional disciples — people who are committed as long as things go the way they think they should. If a controversy blows through the church they are the first to throw in the towel. If a ministry "experience" doesn't fulfill them the way they dreamed it would, they are gone. They say things such as:

> *God placed you in your church for a purpose.*

"If that's the way it's going to be, I may as well leave."

"I don't have to stick around for this kind of thing."

"It's not working out as I thought it would."

"This isn't what I expected when I signed on."

"I just need a break."

Sometimes they leave for no good reason. Maybe they were offended by someone or were not comfortable with a song or style of worship. Usually though, they are simply disappointed when their naive portrait of church life doesn't match reality. They resist the fact that long-term relationships and long-term church success depend on people who weather the good and bad together without bailing out. Provisional disciples don't want to put forth that extra effort. They can appear to be great workers, but it doesn't last. When the task or relationship begins to drag on, they bow out.

The inner circle gave up everything for Jesus and received everything in return.

This happened to Jesus, so it is not surprising that it happens today. John 6:66 says many disciples did not follow Jesus anymore after they had a misunderstanding with Him:

> From that *time* many of his disciples went back, and walked no more with him.

That is the heart and soul of a provisional disciple. In some ways they are the most difficult to incorporate into church life because they are unreliable and unpredictable.

THE INNER CIRCLE

Jesus also had with Him a group of committed disciples. Luke 6:17 (NLT) says, "The disciples stood with Jesus...." This group was there for the long haul. They made things happen. They weathered the good and bad. They made excuses to stay with Jesus rather than desert Him.

The multitude were spectators, and the provisional disciples were temporary or unreliable workers. But the inner circle gave up everything for Jesus and received everything in return.

Their commitment took them on a journey few have ever experienced, full of the power of the Holy Spirit — the dramatic, wonderful presence of God, miracles, signs and wonders.

Every church has (or should have) this inner circle of people who make things happen. They are not perfect Christians, but they are loyal, teachable, humble, and energetic. They make up the core of the church spiritually and in most other areas. They are survivors and thrivers. They make it through tough times.

The inner circle is a wonderful place to be. As in a good marriage, inner-circle people learn to keep commitments, work hard, stay together, and in return, they enjoy depth of character, great friendships, and a stable church.

A successful church moves people into the inner circle where everybody is involved in some way.

Are you in the inner circle? It is not a club, but a place of service. All of us fall into one of these categories. You can probably identify which group you are in.

God placed you in your church for a purpose. You are connected to a specific local body and pastor by design. God wants you to be part of a winning team by working together. The first key is to move from the multitude to the inner circle. A successful church moves people from the multitude into the inner circle. Everybody is involved in some way. Usually the core is a small group, but it does not have to be that way. I believe everybody in a church can be in the inner circle. After all, Jesus sent out another 70 disciples to preach the Kingdom, heal the sick, and cast out demons — not just the 12.

I know a pastor who has no paid pastoral staff members aside from himself, and his church runs 4,000 people in attendance. It works because everybody in the church feels a responsibility to take care of all the jobs that need to be done: bookkeeping, janitorial cleanup, counseling, outreach, youth ministry, choir, and so on. Not only that, the church gives millions of dollars to missions every year. Instead of leaning on paid staff or counting on someone else to pick up the slack, the people have moved into the inner circle and have taken responsibility.

That is a much different picture than you will see at most churches. They may have a large staff but the end result is dismal because few people in the congregation step in to help them. There are many large churches that accomplish very little because they are large in multitude numbers, not inner-circle numbers. They are like lethargic bears with heaps of unused potential.

You cannot have a roaring one-stick fire anymore than you can have a one-straw broom.

It reminds me of an experience I had not long ago when my backyard was overgrown with trees. My wife bought me a chain saw — a subtle hint to start cutting them down. I went out one day and must have cut down a hundred trees. We have a fire pit, and I got permission from the township fire marshal to burn the timber. That afternoon I made a big, beautiful fire with all those sticks and tree branches. It created an astonishing amount of light and heat, even shriveling up the leaves on the surrounding trees that were still standing.

But when I took one piece of burning wood and set it away from the fire, it glowed for a while, then dimmed, and soon went out. The main fire seemed to burn forever, but the individual sticks that tumbled out of it quickly became cold.

That is how it is with your church. Apart from the main fire, you will all be reduced to an ineffective source of light and heat, but together, you can create a massive power source. You cannot have a roaring one-stick fire anymore than you can have a one-straw broom, a one-key piano, or a one-gear car. God created your church to be a soul-winning and disciple-making dynamo in your community. It should be lighting up the whole city! People should come to work on Monday morning talking about what's happening at their church.

Reliable church attendance is the first sign of reliable character.

But it starts with those who get into the inner circle.

QUICK TIPS

How do you get in the inner circle? Here are two ways that will help you immediately:

• NUMBER ONE: MAKE EXCUSES TO BE IN CHURCH.

It is amazing how powerful it is to *be there*. Reliable church attendance, though it sounds routine, is the first sign of reliable character.

Got a headache on Sunday morning? Thank God you're going to church! You can receive prayer. Is it raining on Wednesday night? What a great opportunity to use your new umbrella!

No matter what the pastor is preaching, we should be there. Undoubtedly, the disciples heard some of Jesus' sermons three or four times, but they were there for more than the sermons. They were there to absorb the presence of God. They were there to be of service to Jesus. They were there for those unpredictable moments when God would use them to minister to someone in a way only they could.

What if Kathy had not been in church the day a blind woman, Ruby Jones, visited us? God impressed this inner-circle lay person to pray for Ruby. When she did, Ruby was healed. I only fully believed it when I received a letter from her doctor which read, "This is nothing short of a miracle!"

Going to church is not just about your edification. God may want you to minister to somebody or give a word of encouragement that nobody else can give.

God created your church to be a soul-winning and disciple-making dynamo in your community. It should be lighting up the whole city!

If you are committed to Jesus Christ, the Head of the Church, then you must be committed to His body as well. Paul called the Church "Christ's body." There is no such thing as commitment to the head but not the body. When a man or woman gets married, he or she does not say, "I am committed to your head the rest of my life." We commit to the entire body. Anything less is not real commitment but a charade.

- **NUMBER TWO: DISCOVER YOUR CHURCH'S PRACTICAL NEEDS, AND HELP MEET THEM.**

Ask the pastor or his representative how you can become involved. Sign up to be an usher, a greeter, a parking attendant, a nursery worker. Maybe you will not stay in that ministry long-term, but it will give you a close-up view of what the church needs and what you can do.

If you are in the multitude, move into the inner circle. Don't be just a provisional disciple or part of a multitude that spectates week after week. Put your hand to the plow. Make a commitment and stick with it. That is the first step to helping your pastor succeed.

The second step is learning to be an echo, and that is what we will talk about next.

SUCCESS POINTS:

1. What group are you in: the multitude, the provisional disciples, or the inner circle?

2. What would it take for you to move to the inner circle?

The people of a church need to echo the pastor's vision for the church.

CHAPTER

ECHOING YOUR PASTOR'S VISION

Did you ever have a kid brother or sister trail around after you and repeat everything you said? Maybe you *were* the kid brother or sister. Or maybe in high school you saw groups of guys or girls who followed one person and echoed everything they did or said or wore the same clothes they wore.

The "echo principle" is a critical component of a successful church.

The "echo principle" is more than an annoying or amusing social occurrence; it is a critical component of a successful church. When my son was just a toddler, he tried so hard to echo what his mother and I said. When he saw a motorcycle go by, he said, "What is that?" We said, "Motorcycle," and he said, "Mococycle." I would come home, and he would be sitting on my briefcase in the living room with his cowboy boots on pulling on the handle of my briefcase, and saying, "Mococycle!"

Back then our church was called Mount Hope Assembly, and I asked my son one day what church we went to. He said, "Ma-Poop-And-Sembly." He needed to work on his echo!

SHARING THE VISION

The people of a church need to echo the pastor's vision for the church. You need to become little echoes, kid brothers and sisters repeating God's vision over and over. When you do, you stoke the fires of that vision and make it more intense and powerful.

> *Echo the pastor's vision for the church. It's more valuable than gold.*

Vision is more valuable than gold, and lack of vision is probably the number-one problem from which most churches suffer. Years ago I was invited to speak at a church growth conference. On the final day, there were four or five of us on a panel answering questions posed to us by the attendees. The vast majority of questions were about vision:

"How do you get vision?"

"How do you share vision?"

"Where does vision come from?"

After that day, I began to observe this troubling phenomenon more closely, and I determined in my research that only about 3 percent of all pastors actually have taken the time in prayer and planning to articulate a clear vision. The other 97 percent simply preside over a group and feed the flock. Only a few have a comprehensive picture of where their church is now and where it could be in Christ.

By a miracle of God's grace, I serve as the pastor of Mount Hope Church. When I first became the pastor I had no pastoral background, training, or job skills — nothing. That forced me to study what a pastor does, so I could get it right, and I learned there are three essential things that a pastor is mandated by God to do:

- *Feed the flock.*

- *Protect the flock from wolves that try to destroy it.*

- *Oversee the flock, providing the big picture of where the flock is now and where it needs to go tomorrow and beyond.*

Virtually anybody can preside over a group. I have often told my wife when the pressures of pastoring have been great, how easy it would be to live in a small town and have a church of 200. I could visit a few people during the week, preach on

Sunday, have no Sunday night or Wednesday night services, and do nothing spectacular — just serve as a town minister. The pressure would be off. I would not have any enemies. I would not have to make major decisions or go through colossal building programs.

> *A local church is unified by a common vision set forth by the pastor.*

But that is not the pastor's role. He is not a caretaker in the way that a mortician is, presiding over corpses. He is a vision-caster, a big-picture person, the one shouting, "This way, folks! God is leading us over here!"

In 1 Corinthians 1, Paul wrote about this. The Corinthian church was certainly Pentecostal, but they had all kinds of messy problems. I am glad they did; because in correcting all those problems, Paul left two Holy Spirit inspired letters for us to learn from.

In verse 10 he wrote:

> Now I beseech you, brethren, by the name of our Lord Jesus Christ, that ye all speak the same thing, and *that* there be no divisions among you; but *that* ye be perfectly joined together in the same mind and in the same judgment.

Paul was giving a lesson on the need for unity in being a successful church. Jesus Christ unifies us as a Church universally with brothers and sisters of other denominations. But a local church is unified by something else: A common vision set forth by the pastor.

Jesus does not see your church as what it is but what it can be, indeed, what it should be. Your church may seem small, stuck in debt, and lacking anointing, but Jesus sees a group of world-changers. Remember that He gathered around Himself a ragtag band of tax collectors, fishermen, people who were temperamental and cussed when they got upset; He used them to turn the world upside-down. He looked at Peter and saw not a small acorn but a mighty oak.

He does the same for you and me and for our churches.

FINDING YOUR VISION

Vision is what we see when we look at our life from a bird's-eye view. It is not a mysterious experience that requires falling into a trance or being surrounded by an eerie mist and having a revelation. Most of the time vision is imparted internally by the Lord and becomes a picture of the way things could and should be in the days ahead. It is an interior portrait of conditions that do not yet exist.

When we are discovering and planning our vision, we ask questions such as:

Vision is a portrait of conditions that do not yet exist.

- "What is my purpose?"

- "Where am I going?"

- "How do I get there?"

Churches must do the same thing to find their purpose and move forward, but few people find out what the vision is for their life or their church. Vision marks the difference between those in a growth mode and those in a stagnation mode. Those who are stagnant in their Christian life have failed to see beyond the acorn.

> *Vision marks the difference between those in a growth mode and those in a stagnation mode.*

A church's vision is the responsibility of the pastor. There can be no echo unless there is first a sound. No other person in a church can provide it because God has made vision a specific part of the pastor's portfolio. Other people can sometimes help shape it or confirm it, but true vision must come to a pastor from God. It cannot be copied from a church you read about in a magazine or heard about at a conference.

You would never invest in a company that did not know where it was going. You would ask questions: "What are the strategic plans for the future? What is the big picture? What is the long-term vision?"

If a company representative answers, "We are just floating along, taking things as they come. Whatever fate wants to have happen, will." You would not give them your money. You would not invest in that company.

You would not get on an airplane if you didn't know where it was going. What if you got on a commercial jetliner that was supposed to go to Minneapolis, but the pilot said, "We hope we get to Minneapolis, but depending on which way the wind is blowing, we may end up in Louisiana."

Why would people "get on board" churches that have no vision, do not know where they are going, and do not know what they are called to do?

If the pastor has no articulated vision for the church, no one else will be able to see where the church is going and how they fit in. No one else can make it happen.

A church in Massachusetts was on the decline, and the deacons and trustees got together to vote on making the church a seeker-sensitive church like Willow Creek, a great church near Chicago that reaches thousands of people. The problem was, Willow Creek's vision was for the Chicago area not for the church in Massachusetts. These people felt they needed to control the vision, so they overrode the pastor and began to emulate Willow Creek. They spent money and time, and by the time the project was over, the church was barely alive and almost bankrupt.

There is only one vision for a church, and that vision has to be pursued and sought by the pastor and then shared with the people. God has promised to infuse a church with vision if the people and pastor will only ask.

> Call unto me, and I will answer thee, and shew thee great and mighty things, which thou knowest not.
>
> —Jeremiah 33:3

HOW TO BE AN ECHO

When I found myself as the pastor of Mount Hope Church, I was young, untrained, and excited. My logical inclination was to swing into action and start doing all the traditional things I thought pastors were supposed to do: visit people, have coffee meetings and socials, and find a consensus among the people on what God wanted to do in our church.

But the Holy Spirit spoke to my heart and said, "Wait." So I did. I prayed in the dark hours of the morning when most people were still asleep. I would sit at the altar in the sanctuary with my Bible, a prayer notebook, and a pen, and pray, "God, I don't know how to be a pastor. Will you please be the Pastor of this church? Will you be the Chief Executive Officer, the Chairman of the Board?"

Though there were 226 people on Sunday morning, inside of me I began to *see* a congregation of 1,000 with my eye of faith. And though we were giving only $35,000 a year to missions, I began to *see* us giving a million.

In reality, our attendance stayed in the two hundreds, but I was still seeing 1,000. In my spirit, I *saw* ushers setting up chairs in the aisles to make room for the new visitors. I *saw* bigger buildings, daughter churches, and much more. As I spoke that vision to the people they began to echo it back to me, to each other, and to their neighbors and friends. Soon the city was full of those echoes. The vision was reverberating and stirring people up.

Gradually, the vision came to pass. Sometimes it was so slow; I hardly noticed it. I looked out one day, and the ushers were setting up two rows of chairs in the front, just as I had *seen* in my heart five or six months earlier in prayer. The next thing I knew, we had to go to two services, then three, and then two on Sunday night. We added a balcony for more seats. Traffic was lined up all the way to the highway with cars trying to get into our parking lot.

The vision I had internally was beginning to manifest externally, but it would not have happened if the people of the congregation had not echoed it.

Today over 12,000 people enjoy membership at Mount Hope Church, here and in our branch and satellite churches. My vision keeps expanding, and now I'm seeing over 30,000 people in my faith vision.

OPPOSITION

Vision brings success, but it also brings opposition, and this is a major area where you can help your pastor. When he receives a vision from God, begin to echo that vision the best you can. Talk about it, pray about it, show up at meetings, and lend practical support. Some people will surely begin to oppose that vision, and unless the church fights for it, the vision can be lost.

I remember the day a deacon pulled me aside and told me to stop raising people's hopes by casting visions and dreams all the time. Instead of echoing my vision, he was acting like a sound-absorbent wall. He was trying to extinguish the vision God had for the church.

Then I heard that preachers around Lansing were speaking out against me from their pulpits because they felt threatened by our church's big vision. I would turn on the local radio and hear sermons preached against me. They did not want to echo God's vision but reject it, and even try to squash it.

When a pastor receives a vision, there will be questions, criticism, skepticism. The pastor's job is to keep casting the vision, and the people's job is to keep echoing it, even during opposition.

I remember one of the greatest trials of my ministry. A deacon had verbally ripped me apart saying nobody would believe my vision. He called me everything, including a false prophet. He said my sermons did not reach people and that no one was being fed. He did this in front of my secretary, my associate, and fellow board members.

That night I decided to get better — not bitter. I stayed at the church that night and prayed. Between 10:00 and 11:00 p.m., God spoke to two men who were church members and told them I was at the church praying. They walked in the back door and said, "God told us to come over here and hold up your arms."

You can't imagine how good it was to see them! It felt as if I had found a refreshing oasis. Together we prayed, and I kept casting my vision from that day on. The people of the church echoed it, and the vision continued to grow.

The deacon resigned and quit the church. He missed the greatest revival of church growth, evangelism, and discipleship to ever sweep through our city!

SUCCESS POINTS:

1. What is your pastor's vision?

2. How can you echo that vision?

3. How can you support it in practical ways?

*W*olves are out there
and they try to disrupt the
vision of a church.

CHAPTER

WATCHING OUT FOR WOLVES

One of the biggest hindrances to a pastor's vision is not apathy or laziness but wolves in sheep's clothing.

This is a hard fact for normal churchgoers to understand. They think everyone who comes to church must have pure motives. After all, we all smile and greet each other and shake hands in the foyer.

But wolves are a fact of life. You see wolf problems popping up throughout the Gospels and in Paul's writings. In Acts 20:28-30 Paul said to the pastors of the Ephesian church:

> Take heed therefore unto yourselves, and to all the flock, over the which the Holy Ghost hath made you overseers, to feed the church of God, which he hath purchased with his own blood.
>
> For I know this, that after my departing shall grievous wolves enter in among you, not sparing the flock.

Also of your own selves shall men arise, speaking perverse things, to draw away disciples after them.

"Perverse" refers to people who come into the church and twist the pastor's words.

I looked up the word *perverse*. It refers to people who come into the church and twist the pastor's words. It means to deliberately misinterpret. It has its roots in what Paul called "the mystery of iniquity" which would foreshadow the coming Antichrist.

WOLVES DON'T ECHO

It is the pastor's responsibility to spot wolves, and God gives pastors supernatural discernment in this area. I have seen it time and time again. Many people who were once key workers in our church have left and are totally backslidden today. They bar-hop, divorce their wives, run around with other former believers, and are now living on the scrap heap of life. In *every* instance, they did not echo the pastor's vision. They wanted a political church or a church that was more this way or that way. They did not echo the pastor's vision, and they became wolves instead of sheep in the flock of God.

A man came to my office one day and said, "Pastor, they threw me out of the Helps Department, and they don't want me in the Care Department anymore, and for some reason, the Music Ministry doesn't want me either. Even though you are anointed, the guys leading these departments do not have what it takes because they don't recognize the anointing on my life. You hired some real clowns."

I responded the only way I know how. I said, "I prayed through the decisions to bring those men on staff. If they are clowns, I must be the master clown."

"Oh no," he said, "you are not the master clown. You are anointed. In fact, I see rain from Heaven falling on you every time you preach."

Whenever people try to butter me up, alarm bells start going off inside me. They always have butter in one hand and a sharp knife in the other.

This man said in a super-spiritual tone, "I am here to tell you I want to work for you personally. God told me I am called to be your watchdog, to spot when members start getting into worldliness. I'll let you know when somebody gets off track."

I responded, "You are called to be a 'watchdog,' huh? Have you ever read the end of the book of Revelation and discovered where dogs are found? The Bible says they are outside the gate, not inside the gate."

Anytime a wolf talks bad about a pastor or church, I know for a fact he or she is failing to deal with a sin.

He stormed off, left the church, and went to "bless" somebody else. I was happy to see him go. He was a divider who thought he was a uniter. He had his own agenda in which his personal "so-called ministry" played the chief role. He did not echo the pastor's vision because he was so full of his own selfish vision.

HOW TO IDENTIFY WOLVES

It is very common to come across wolves who try to split a church's vision. They are easy to spot:

1. THEY PRETEND TO BE IN THE KNOW OR HAVE SOME SORT OF INSIDE INFORMATION.

They say, for example, "I used to be in a position of authority, and I know something that nobody else knows. I even have documentation."

2. THEY CLAIM TO BE CLOSER TO GOD THAN OTHER PEOPLE THOUGH THEIR BEHAVIOR DOES NOT SHOW IT.

They say, "I pray two hours a day now instead of one. I am hearing from God all the time."

3. THEY SPEAK OUT OF BITTERNESS THOUGH THEY TRY TO DISGUISE IT WITH SO-CALLED GOOD INTENTIONS.

First John 4:1 says we can test the spirits and see if they are of God. The Holy Spirit will show you who is speaking out of bitterness.

4. THEY CLAIM SUPERIOR, SUPERNATURAL WISDOM.

The book of James calls it earthly, sensual, and demonic wisdom. These people have actually attracted demonic forces to their lives because of their hidden rebellion, and their wisdom becomes demonic. In fact, the Bible says that their lamps will be put out, which means they are at a point where they do not know the difference between the voice of God and the voice of the devil.

> But if ye have bitter envying and strife in your hearts, glory not, and lie not against the truth. This wisdom descendeth not from above, but *is* earthly, sensual, devilish. For where envying and strife *is*, there *is* confusion and every evil work.
>
> —James 3:14-16
>
> ...but the lamp of the wicked shall be put out.
>
> —Proverbs 13:9b

5. THEY DO NOT HAVE THE BEST INTEREST OF THE FLOCK AT HEART ALTHOUGH THEY CLAIM THEY DO.

They will affirm that they have the best interest of the church at heart then proceed to gossip or slander someone. They literally become pawns of Satan without realizing it.

6. THEY ALMOST ALWAYS HAVE SOME SIN THEY ARE NOT DEALING WITH WHICH CAUSES THEM TO LOSE ALL DISCERNMENT.

Anytime a wolf talks bad about a pastor or church, I know for a fact he or she is failing to deal with a sin. I have found this to be 100 percent accurate.

7. YOU WILL NOT FIND THEM INVOLVED IN THE REAL SPIRITUAL LIFE OF THE CHURCH OTHER THAN FOR SHOW.

They say they know everything about the vision of God and what people are doing, but you do not usually find them at the regular prayer meetings or in the church's intercessory prayer times. Their spiritual times are "too deep" to participate in a "shallow corporate prayer meeting."

Perhaps you have seen wolves in action, or maybe you have never had the displeasure of dealing with them, but as a pastor I can tell you they are out there and they try to disrupt the vision of a church. They want to silence the echoes and smother the pastor's vision.

WHAT WOLVES GET

Early in Oral Roberts' ministry, three men saw his success and realized there was an opportunity to make financial gain. They came to him privately after a crusade and said, "Brother Roberts, we know God's hand is on you. Things are really happening in your ministry and we also know you are collecting an awful lot of money in these meetings."

That is a very common sign of wolves. They like to talk about money just as Judas Iscariot said:

> Why was not this ointment sold for three hundred pence, and given to the poor?
>
> —John 12:5

Oral Roberts told the men, "God told me to never touch the glory or the gold that belongs to Him."

They said, "If you do not let us in on the financial end, we are going to ruin your ministry."

And that is what they tried to do. They spread rumors about Roberts, some of which persist even to this day. They cast doubt over his character and created so much confusion he had to shut down his crusade and move to another state: Oklahoma.

Several months later, Roberts was holding a crusade, and an emaciated man came through the healing line, sunken-cheeked and shaking. He looked up and said, "Brother Roberts, will you forgive me?" Roberts recognized him as one of the three men who had spread the rumors. He reached out his hand and said, "I forgive you," and God healed the man. He became a good friend of Roberts and later served on the Board of Regents at Oral Roberts University.

> *The best way to help our church advance is by echoing the vision.*

The other two men became diseased and died untimely deaths.

THE UNSTOPPABLE VISION

God's vision will not be stopped. People will come and go, but His work will go forward. We must be mindful of this and grab hold of what God is doing. He doesn't need us, but we desperately need Him. And the best way to help our church advance is by echoing the vision.

What is the vision God has given your pastor for your church? I know the vision God has given my church. I see a church of loving, dedicated disciples of Jesus Christ who want to hear the Word, preach the Gospel, and take as many people as possible to Heaven.

As it turns out, there are many people in my city who want to echo my vision. We have gone from 226 people in Sunday services to over 4,000 in Lansing and 8,000 more in our branch, missions, and satellite churches. By the grace of God, we give more than two million dollars to missions every year.

- We had a vision for a chapel that would serve as a prayer retreat, so we built our Garden Prayer Chapel.

- We had a vision for a workout place, so we built a Youth Action Center, a Health and Fitness Spa, and a huge double gym.

- We had a vision to plant churches, and now we have twenty-some Mount Hope Churches across Michigan, and fifteen more around the world.

- We had a vision for a leadership training institute. Now we have a first-class, fully accredited institute training hundreds of students for full-time ministry.

- We had a vision to provide housing to widows who otherwise would live in dangerous neighborhoods. Soon we will have Anna's House where widows can live in safe, self-contained apartments.

- We had a vision of a place for senior citizens and soon Caleb's Retirement Village will be complete.

- We had a vision to see the sick healed spiritually, emotionally, and physically, and now we have the multimillion dollar Gilead Healing Center. Medical doctors who use integrative methods and Care Pastors are on duty to help people.

- We shared a vision for reaching the at-risk children of our city. Today, buses go out every weekend picking up hundreds of children living in the city housing developments.

- We wanted to provide housing to missionaries on furlough so they don't have to spend thousands on rent, so we have Mercy House Apartments where missionaries and ministers can stay at no cost to them.

- We built our vision of a 24-hour Global Prayer Center where intercessory prayer constantly goes before God's throne night and day.

We see so much more ahead, and I believe those visions will come to pass, too, because the people in our church echo the pastor's vision.

But vision alone cannot move a church forward. There is another vital ingredient that must be active. We will find out what that is in the next chapter.

SUCCESS POINTS:

1. What do wolves try to do to a church's vision?

2. How can you help your pastor overcome the work of wolves?

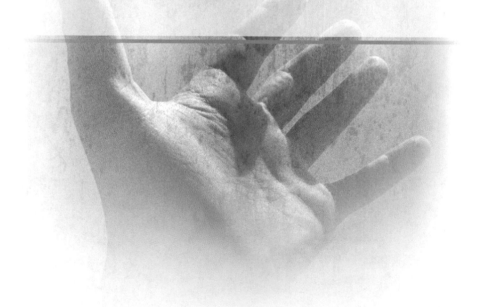

U*nity is of primary
importance in helping your
pastor succeed.*

CHAPTER

ENDEAVORING TO KEEP UNITY

If we compare a church to an automobile, vision is the "gasoline;" the fuel that makes it go forward. But there is another component that is just as important. It is the oil that keeps an engine running smoothly and at the right temperature. That "oil" is one of the most powerful tools in God's Kingdom. Paul wrote about it in Ephesians 4:1-13.

> I therefore, the prisoner of the Lord, beseech you that ye walk worthy of the vocation wherewith ye are called,
>
> With all lowliness and meekness, with longsuffering, forbearing one another in love; Endeavouring to keep the unity of the Spirit in the bond of peace.
>
> *There is* one body, and one Spirit, even as ye are called in one hope of your calling; One Lord, one faith, one

baptism, One God and Father of all, who *is* above all, and through all, and in you all.

But unto every one of us is given grace according to the measure of the gift of Christ. Wherefore he saith, When he ascended up on high, he led captivity captive, and gave gifts unto men.

(Now that he ascended, what is it but that he also descended first into the lower parts of the earth? He that descended is the same also that ascended up far above all heavens, that he might fill all things.)

And he gave some, apostles; and some, prophets; and some, evangelists; and some, pastors and teachers; For the perfecting of the saints, for the work of the ministry, for the edifying of the body of Christ: Till we all come in the unity of the faith, and of the knowledge of the Son of God, unto a perfect man, unto the measure of the stature of the fullness of Christ.

What is this powerful substance, this "oil" for the engine of a church? It is unity in the Spirit and unity of the faith.

UNITY

Unity takes individuals and turns them into powerful teams. It binds our energies and abilities together into a massive source of power.

Think of the greatest sports teams in football, basketball, baseball, or hockey. The championship teams are not always those with the most stars but those teams that band together into a fighting unit. Every year you see a franchise spend millions of dollars to acquire skilled players, but when the season starts, it is clear that the team has not "jelled." The players may be talented individually, but they have not pooled their strengths to produce a unified team.

Maybe you have worked for a corporation or business and seen the power of unity. When a management team works together and the other employees get on board and support them, a company becomes unstoppable. But when there is disunity, fractiousness, and competing visions, a company is doomed.

Unity takes individuals and turns them into powerful teams.

The same is true of families. When a family has unity, they can accomplish virtually anything they set their minds on.

Churches, too, run on the oil of unity. In fact, the Bible uses oil as a symbol for unity when it says:

> Behold, how good and how pleasant *it is* for brethren to dwell together in unity! *It is* like the precious ointment upon the head, that ran down upon the beard, *even* Aaron's beard: that went down to the skirts of his garments.
>
> —Psalm 133:1-2

When a church is in unity, its power grows exponentially to ten, fifty, or a hundred times what it was. Maybe you are a part of a church in unity and see the marvelous things that are being accomplished.

The first-century church experienced unity on the day of Pentecost (Acts 2). Earlier Jesus told 500 people to wait for the promise of the Father in Jerusalem, but after ten days, only 120 remained. Maybe the other 380 broke unity. We don't know. But the ones who kept unity received much more than they could have anticipated. The sound of a mighty rushing wind roared into that upper room, and they were all filled with the Holy Spirit and began to speak with other tongues as the Spirit of God gave utterance. Tongues of fire appeared on their heads. Peter went outside and preached a simple message, and 3,000 people came to Christ.

When a church is unified, its power grows exponentially.

That is the power of unity!

In the Old Testament, when Solomon's temple was ready to be dedicated, the glory of God filled the place so strongly that the priests were not able to enter the temple to minister (2 Chronicles 7:1-3). They had unity, and it brought tremendous power into their midst.

WHAT UNITY ISN'T

When we talk about unity, we are not talking about the mind science cult called Unity, nor are we talking about uniformity. I attended a church where all the men wore black suits and the women wore their hair down to their knees. They all looked like twins. They sought unity by looking alike, but that is not what the Bible means by unity.

Unity is not ecumenicalism or syncretism, where we try to have unity with everybody who believes in God, including

Buddhists, Hindus, and Muslims. There is no fellowship between Christ and demons and no unity between Christianity and religions founded on the doctrines of demons.

Nor does unity mean nobody ever complains. Christian unity is not Communist-style conformity but rather a pervading love that is maintained even when differences come up. For example, in the book of Acts, some of the believers complained to the church leaders because the Hebrew widows were being overlooked in the distribution of food. That complaint brought about a systematic change that helped organize the church in a better way. Pointing out problems is not breaking unity, but it depends on the spirit in which it is done.

True unity is beautifully represented by an orchestra. Not all musicians in an orchestra play the same instruments. Some play wind instruments, some percussion, some stringed instruments. And not all instruments are playing the same part, but they are playing one song in perfect harmony. That is the Bible's picture of unity.

THE BENEFITS OF UNITY

A minister I know was scheduled to be a guest speaker at a church. Before he arrived, the church members met and said, "We are going to stay in agreement and pray for these meetings." That is what they did. When the minister arrived to speak, he found people in great unity. As they were worshiping God, it was as if a cloud came and hovered over the people's heads just as in Solomon's day. Nobody in the church could remain standing, and every person there who did not know Jesus Christ got saved. Every sick person was healed, and every demonically bound person was set free. It was the greatest service this friend of mine had ever seen.

Another minister and his congregation decided to stay in complete unity and pray for unsaved loved ones. I am sure there were all kinds of temptations to get out of unity, but they hung together and prayed for 85 people over the course of two weeks. By the end of that time, all but two had accepted Jesus Christ.

Unity helps churches accomplish their God-given goals. When I was a bachelor, I bought a little two-bedroom house on a dead-end street. Then I got married, and before we knew it, my wife and I had two children. We were a happy family, but our house was too small.

> *Unity helps churches accomplish their God-given goals.*

My wife and I took a piece of paper and wrote out a prayer of agreement. Together we decided we needed at least three bedrooms; we preferred a certain location and so forth. We prayed that prayer of agreement every night before going to bed. All of us, including the children, would say, "Thank you, Jesus, for our new house." One day our agent called and said, "The perfect house for you just came on the market." We drove by, and I called back and said, "We'll take it."

Unity in prayer and purpose helped us achieve our goal for a larger house to suit our growing family.

UNSPOKEN REQUESTS

I have never understood people who give unspoken requests. I was visiting a church one day, and the pastor, recognizing me, asked me to lead in prayer. So we went around the sanctuary and took prayer requests. The first person said he had a "special unspoken," but I thought he said he wanted prayer for "a special on smokin'." I thought it was strange to request a "special on smoking," but I said we would remember the brother in prayer. Someone else stood up and said, "I want to request prayer for a special on smokin' too." Her hair was up in a bun, and I could hardly believe she was a smoker. One after another, people asked for prayer for a special on smoking, and I thought, "This church has a lot of smokers."

Unity in prayer and purpose helped us achieve our goal.

The pastor said, "Brother Williams, lead us in prayer," and I said, "You bet I will. Father, in the Name of Jesus, I pray for all these people who are bound by tobacco. Even the pastor's wife has this problem. Let today be the day of deliverance for all of them. Amen."

As I was praying, I heard a rustling as if people were uncomfortable. The pastor thanked me, and afterward I said to him in private, "I cannot believe so many people in the church smoke." He said, "What do you mean?" I said, "All those people requesting the special on smokin'."

He said, "They were saying *'special unspoken.'*"

"What does *that* mean?" I asked.

He said, "It means they do not want to tell anybody what their prayer request is, but they want prayer for it all the same."

That was my introduction to "unspoken requests," and I continue to question their value. It seems to me that true unity must have a subject. How can you agree with someone about an unspoken request? Of course, not every setting is appropriate to mention all of our prayer needs, but the Bible says to confess our sins one to another (James 5:16). At some point we need to tell someone our need and let them unite with us in prayer. I doubt that praying about "unspoken requests" is nearly as powerful as uniting in prayer against a known enemy.

> *Several things hinder unity, and each of them can be avoided.*

HINDRANCES TO UNITY

Several things hinder unity, and each of them can be resolved:

1. MISUNDERSTANDINGS.

These are unavoidable. They happen in homes and churches. It happened in Jesus' ministry (John 6:56-66) when He told His disciples they would have to eat His flesh and drink His blood or they would have no part of Him. Many thought, "Gross! Eat His flesh, drink His blood? We are out of here." They misunderstood what picture He was painting. The tragic thing is that all they had to do was ask, "What did you mean when you said 'eat your flesh and drink your blood?'" He might have given them a picture of Holy Communion and what was coming in the future, but they did not bother to ask what He was talking about. They let the misunderstanding create a breach of unity.

Striving always breaks unity. It breeds an argumentative spirit.

2. PERCEIVED RIGHTS.

When we come to Jesus Christ, we give up our rights. I have seen people grow up in the church, and because their great-grandfather was an elder or deacon, they feel they have a right to direct the church. Sometimes they want to steer the congregation in the way they want to go, and this breaks unity.

3. NOT HANDLING OFFENSES PROPERLY.

When we are offended by a fellow believer, unity will be broken unless we handle the offense correctly. (See Matthew 18:15-18.)

4. STRIVING.

The Bible says in 2 Timothy 2:5 that the servant of the Lord must not strive. Striving, a fleshly grasping after power, wealth, or influence, always breaks unity. It breeds an argumentative spirit.

Absalom was a striver. He sat at the gate of the city and stirred people up against his father, King David. Pretty soon he had enough people who sympathized with him, and they rose up to overthrow the kingdom. But in time, those people were also overthrown. Absalom was riding his horse through the woods, and his long hair got caught in a tree branch. The horse left him hanging by his hair, and a man named Joab took three daggers and shoved them through his heart (2 Samuel 18:9-14). Absalom was trapped by the devil because of strife.

David, on the other hand, would not touch King Saul because he was anointed by God. David did not strive for power. He had all kinds of opportunities to bring disunity to Israel, but he would not do it.

WHAT PROMOTES UNITY

Several things help us to keep unity:

1. UNDERSTANDING AUTHORITY.

Authority is hard for some people to understand. God has raised up authority in homes, the workplace, and the church. We are all equal as brothers and sisters in Christ, but in the church God has given authority to different people. I am not on a power kick, but *I am* recognizing the system God has put in place. In His grace He raises up pastors and expects them to use their authority to lead. Sometimes the use of that authority ruffles feathers.

For example, at one point in our church, there was a gifted and talented man. We began to notice things about his ministry:

- He was entering into bizarre teachings.

- He was gathering a following after himself and not after Christ.

- His moral level had deteriorated.

- There was a big integrity gap in his life.

When we realized these things, I decided to remove him from leadership. All of his followers were upset because I was not "spiritual enough" to understand his deep, bizarre teaching. I received a letter from a lady asking how I could remove this man from leadership. "After all, he prayed for people, and they were healed." I wrote her back and said, "It boils down to this. Either I am your pastor or I am not. God has given me oversight over the whole church. The pastor sees the "whole pie." You see one sliver of the pie. I made a decision based on the "whole pie." If you do not trust me as your shepherd, then I thank you for the years you have worshiped here, and I wish you God's best in finding another church."

Prayer is an incredible unifier. Nothing knits spirits together like prayer.

That shook her up. She expected me to say, "I'm sorry. We will put him back in leadership and let him spread his venom to others."

She came to my office and apologized. The church went forward at a much healthier pace, and as a much healthier place, after that man was out of leadership.

2. UNITED PRAYER.

I have heard many pastors say they cannot get their deacons to come to prayer meetings. I say, "Then why are they deacons?" Put the gavel down. Pastor, exercise your God-given authority. Make it mandatory that anyone in leadership must attend prayer meetings.

Why? Because prayer is an incredible unifier. After praying together, you love everybody and feel like hugging the nastiest people you know. Nothing knits spirits together like prayer.

3. HANDLING OFFENSES PROPERLY.

If somebody said or did something that upset me, it would be wrong for me to try to "work it out with the Lord." It is more scriptural to go to the person who has offended you, explain the offense, and reconcile with them. Jesus said:

> Therefore if thou bring thy gift to the altar, and there rememberest that thy brother hath ought against thee; Leave there thy gift before the altar, and go thy way; first be reconciled to thy brother, and then come and offer thy gift.
>
> —Matthew 5:23-24

It is nearly impossible to keep quiet about an offense. If you don't go to the person who offended you, you will probably go to someone else, and that is where Satan traps people alive. He turns good Christians in to gossips. Better to speak our heart in private to the person we believe wronged us, or who believes we've wronged them, than spread poison to others.

Unity is of primary importance in helping your pastor succeed. If a church is not flowing in unity it does not matter what spiritual gifts people have. Nothing can stand on a wobbly foundation.

The first half of this book has been about building a solid group of people who are eager and willing to work together — who share the same vision, resist the work of wolves, and insist on maintaining unity. With that in place, we can move on to the other critically important ways you can help your pastor and church succeed starting with finding your unique place in the church.

SUCCESS POINTS:

1. How do you, as an individual, promote unity in your church?

2. What has your church accomplished by being unified?

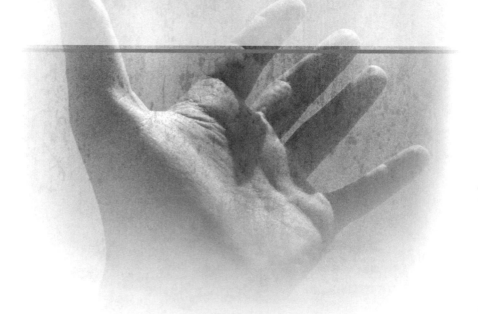

Y*our unique place in your church is directly related to the spiritual gifts God has given you.*

CHAPTER 5

FINDING YOUR
UNIQUE PLACE

So far we have talked about:

• Moving from the multitude to the inner circle

• Echoing the pastor's vision

• Watching out for wolves

• Keeping unity

In this chapter I am going to show you how to find your unique place in your church.

Each of us wants to know where we fit into our church body. Are we supposed to work in the nursery? The singles' ministry? The outreach ministry? Drive buses? Bring snacks? Teach Sunday school? We know God has outfitted us for a task, and we feel empty until we discover what it is.

Your unique place in your church is directly related to the spiritual gifts God has given you. You were not born with a random assortment of talents but with very specific talents that relate to your personality and your life's destiny. When you were born again, you received spiritual gifts too — talents that are intended to help the church.

> For as we have many members in one body, and all members have not the same office: So we, *being* many, are one body in Christ, and every one members one of another. Having then gifts differing according to the grace that is given to us, whether prophecy, *let us prophesy* according to the proportion of faith.
>
> —Romans 12:4-6

> To whom coming, *as unto* a living stone, disallowed indeed of men, but chosen of God, *and* precious, Ye also, as lively stones, are built up a spiritual house, an holy priesthood, to offer up spiritual sacrifices, acceptable to God by Jesus Christ.
>
> —1 Peter 2:4-5

> As every man hath received the gift, *even so* minister the same one to another, as good stewards of the manifold grace of God.
>
> —1 Peter 4:10

SUPERNATURAL

God's gifts are supernatural. Discovering them is the only way you will find lasting fulfillment in your Christian service and the only way your church will fully succeed.

God wants to partner with you. You do the natural; God does the super, and the result is supernatural. Without the "super" part, the church simply becomes another social club. Without the supernatural, we cannot meet people's deepest needs.

That is why some churches never see people born again, never see miracles, never see dramatic life changes. The prophet Ezekiel wrote about a time when this happened. Everybody came to the temple and did what they believed to be worship. They prayed and worked at the temple but they lacked true devotion and true spirituality. So God said, "My glory is leaving Jerusalem." (See Ezekiel 8-11.) When it did, nobody realized it. Everything appeared to go on in the same way. They were so involved in the natural that they forgot to pay attention to the "super."

> *God wants to partner with you. You do the natural, God does the super, and the result is supernatural.*

And what about Samson? The Spirit of the Lord left him, and he didn't even realize it (Judges 16:20).

The Bible speaks of priests who claimed to be relying on the Lord, spouting off, "The Lord is here among us," when He really wasn't (Micah 3:11).

We can organize a church, but unless God turns it into a living organism built by living stones, we have nothing more than a human institution. Spiritual gifts, in a sense, bring the embodiment of Christ to earth. If there is no presence of God in our meeting, we cannot call ourselves a church. Church is where God is working to confirm His Word, with signs following.

I heard a story about a construction worker who hurt his thumb on the job. The foreman said for him to go to the medical clinic, so the man walked through the door of the clinic, and there was nothing in the room but two doors. One door said, "Illness," the other said, "Injury." He went through the "Injury" door and found himself in another room with two doors; one that said, "Internal," and one that said, "External." He looked at his smashed thumb and walked through the "External" door into another empty room with two more doors marked, "Therapy" and "Treatment." He went through the "Treatment" door into yet another empty room with two doors marked, "Minor" and "Major." He walked through the door marked "Minor" and found himself back on the street.

Every one of us receives a special gift and call.

When the man returned to the job site, the foreman asked if he had gotten any help. He answered, "Not really, but that is the best organized outfit I have ever seen."

That is what people might say about your church if there is plenty of organization, but no spiritual help available. The best organized church in the world might as well be torn down if it is not helping people in a supernatural way.

You Are Called

Usually when a church fails, it is because people have not been given opportunities to use their unique gifts; to spread their wings and fly.

You are a living stone, called by God to be part of the spiritual temple called the Church.

> And now God is building you, as living stones, into his spiritual temple.
>
> —1 Peter 2:5a (NLT)

1. You have a gift, a ministry in the church.

Every one of us receives a special gift and call the minute we come to Christ, and the diversity of gifts is wonderful. No two people's set of gifts are alike. For example, our church has a ministry called "Clowns for Christ." Not everybody can do that. Some cook for shut-ins, help people with their taxes, or clean up yards for the disabled.

2. Your calling and gifts are irrevocable, according to Romans 11:29.

God has given you a gift, and He is not going to withdraw it. You can sit on a pew and never use that gift, but God will not withdraw it. If you do not willingly become part of your spiritual temple, there is going to be a gap.

3. There is contentment and success when we find and use our gift from God.

Some people are greeters and have a supernatural ministry of making people feel welcome. Those same people do not feel comfortable praying with people at the altars. And, altar ministers might not feel comfortable greeting people at the doors. When we find our niche, we feel energized and successful.

FINDING YOUR UNIQUE PLACE

How do you discover *your* niche in the church?

1. LEARN ALL YOU CAN ABOUT THE GIFTS AND MINISTRIES GOD HAS GIVEN TO THE CHURCH.

Get a copy of my book, *Gifts That Shape Your Life and Change Your World,* or another book that will lead you through a process of discovery. Attend a seminar or class to guide you through the process. The more you know, the quicker you will find your place.

2. PAY ATTENTION TO THE INNER TUG.

For it is God which worketh in you both to will and to do of *his* good pleasure.

—Philippians 2:13

If you have an inner tug toward a certain ministry or certain gift, perhaps it is God speaking to you about it.

Years ago I felt a strong desire to preach and teach God's Word. I would walk to work and preach all the way. I was leading a Bible study at my house using cassette tapes, and one day the people who attended said, "We would like you to teach us instead of playing Bible tapes every week." So I agreed. I didn't think my teaching was very good, but they wanted me to do it again, so I became a Bible-study teacher.

That is where I started teaching, but it was preceded and confirmed by an inner tug.

That inner tug, which is really the Holy Spirit speaking to us, can lead us in many wonderful discoveries. One night my wife and I were at a crusade in Detroit, and there was a young boy whom we had met who was going to walk home that night. We offered him a ride, and while we were in the car the Lord told me to give the boy the biggest bill I had in my pocket. I had a couple of bills, and I pulled out the biggest one, and when we reached his home, which was in an awful neighborhood, I put that bill in his hand. "What is this for?" he asked, and instantly God gave me a divine fragment of knowledge and I said, "It's to buy your mother a birthday present."

He started crying and asked how I knew it was his mother's birthday. He said he wanted so much to buy her something, but he didn't have any money. The only way I could have known was through the inner tug.

> *That inner tug, which is really the Holy Spirit speaking to us, can lead us in many wonderful discoveries.*

Another time while preaching, I kept seeing an image of an abscessed tooth in my mind. I didn't know what to do about it. Was it knowledge from God or was I remembering some aspirin commercial I had seen? At the end of my message, I prayed, "Thank you, Lord, for your Word, and if anybody has an abscessed tooth, I pray that you will heal it right now." At that moment a lady in the second row jumped up and ran out of the sanctuary. I did not know if I had offended her, but after the service ended, she came back and said, "Pastor, when you prayed for that abscessed tooth, I was in miserable pain, and I felt a hot flash go through my tooth and instantly the pain was gone. I ran to the ladies' room to look, and all the swelling and infection is gone."

> *Do what you enjoy and it will become a source of strength for you.*

Since that time, I have learned to pay attention to the inner tug. It has grown within me; an inner voice that leads, warns, and provides wisdom. I have sometimes seen the motives behind certain people's requests or actions. I have been able to foresee certain problems coming into an individual's life and certain dangers our church must avoid.

You can trust this same leading of the Holy Spirit to help you find your place in the church.

3. ASK YOURSELF, "DO I ENJOY WHERE I AM SERVING?"

The Bible says, "...for the joy of the LORD is your strength" (Nehemiah 8:10b). If you are miserable greeting people, maybe that is not your call. Do what you enjoy and it will become a source of strength for you.

4. ARE OTHER PEOPLE BLESSED BY YOUR MINISTRY?

I encourage people to try out their gift and see what

benefit it brings. If no one is blessed, perhaps you have chosen the wrong area of ministry. If you sign up for the nursery and are grumpy the whole time, I doubt that anyone else is enjoying your ministry.

If you want to sing a solo but people wince when you hit the high notes, perhaps you should reconsider that gift.

If you prophesy and nobody is blessed by your prophecies, you are probably not called to prophesy.

Speaking of prophecy, I have heard some humdingers in my time. One man said, "Have I not said unto thee, 'Happy trails to you?'" I thought it was Roy Rogers who said that, not God! I have heard many prophecies that bless nobody. The New Testament says prophecy edifies, builds up, comforts, and strengthens. If that doesn't happen, maybe that is not your gift.

5. IS IT FOR A GREATER CAUSE THAN YOURSELF?

Spiritual gifts are not given so we can promote ourselves, gather a following after ourselves, or profit personally. These gifts are for the benefit of others. A test of maturity is how you use your gift once you discover what it is.

6. DO NOT DESPISE THE DAY OF SMALL BEGINNINGS.

Great ministries start small. Every great preacher, Billy Graham included, started out preaching to half-empty churches and small crowds.

> For who hath despised the day of small things?
>
> —Zechariah 4:10a

I am amazed by the number of people who walk through the door of our church and think I am going to make them assistant pastors when they are not willing to start small.

Spiritual gifts are not given so we can promote ourselves. These gifts are for the benefit of others.

7. BE FAITHFUL.

This is how small ministries grow. If you are faithful in the small things, the Lord will give you charge over greater things (Matthew 25:21). A man said to me, "I am leaving the church. I cannot break into leadership here; it is all closed up." I said, "My brother, you never break into leadership at Mount Hope Church. You grow into leadership."

Promotion comes not from the east or the west but from the Lord Himself. When He wants to promote you, nobody can stop it.

> The LORD maketh poor, and maketh rich: he bringeth low, and lifteth up.
>
> —1 Samuel 2:7

If you are a Christian, you have a unique place and a unique set of gifts that God wants to use. These steps will help you find your place in the church.

There is another area of life that can directly affect your ministry. Success in this area will help your pastor more than any other way. Yet, few people make the connection between what I am about to discuss and their effectiveness in ministry. Let's see what it is.

SUCCESS POINTS:

1. Do you know what your spiritual gifts are?

2. How are you using your gifts in your church?

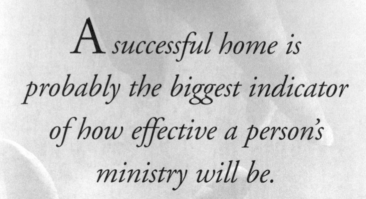

A *successful home is
probably the biggest indicator
of how effective a person's
ministry will be.*

CHAPTER

DEVELOPING A SUCCESSFUL CHRISTIAN HOME

It was Mom's birthday, and the kids told her to stay in bed because they wanted to do something special. She began to smell bacon and eggs and heard them rustling around in the kitchen. Any minute she knew they would come up the stairs and deliver breakfast in bed.

Time passed. Eventually, the kids called for her and she came downstairs to discover them eating bacon and eggs and pancakes at the table. They said, "For your birthday, we decided to cook our own breakfast."

If you want to help your church succeed, develop a successful Christian home in spite of obstacles. Research shows

HOW TO HELP YOUR PASTOR SUCCEED

that people who complain about their church almost always have problems at home. I have found this to be true almost without fail. When a church member cannot be pleased there is usually a problem in the home. When someone gets angry and leaves the church, it is not uncommon to hear that he or she was divorced soon after that.

From a pastor's viewpoint, a successful home is probably the biggest indicator of how effective a person's ministry will be. When people lack stability in the home, even if they are enthusiastic volunteers, their ministry is usually stunted. Healthy families are the bedrock of a healthy church and a clear gauge of a church's potential.

Healthy families are the bedrock of a healthy church.

GROWING A SUCCESSFUL FAMILY

Paul adopted Timothy as a spiritual son because Timothy's father was a nonbeliever. In 2 Timothy 1, starting in verse three, Paul wrote:

> I thank God, whom I serve from *my* forefathers with pure conscience, that without ceasing I have remembrance of thee in my prayers night and day; Greatly desiring to see thee, being mindful of thy tears...
>
> —2 Timothy 1:3-4a

Timothy's tears may have been for his father, wanting him to be a Christian, to have faith as his mother Eunice had.

...that I may be filled with joy; When I call to remembrance the unfeigned faith that is in thee, which dwelt first in thy grandmother Lois, and thy mother Eunice; and I am persuaded that in thee also.

—2 Timothy 1:4b-5

Timothy's grandmother had faith in Christ, and she passed that faith on to her daughter Eunice who passed it on to Timothy.

Wherefore I put thee in remembrance that thou stir up the gift of God, which is in thee by the putting on of my hands. For God hath not given us the spirit of fear; but of power, and of love, and of a sound mind.

—2 Timothy 1:6-7

This passage lays the groundwork for recommendations I want to share with you. I believe the following advice is powerful enough to keep your family rooted, balanced, and in love with each other and God.

• NUMBER ONE: PRAY.

As Paul adopted Timothy, he prayed for him. In prayer we feel tenderness of heart for the people we pray for, especially family members. In a successful home, the husband and wife pray for each other, the children pray for their parents and for each other, and the parents pray for the children. I am unaware of anything that bonds families quicker and with more lasting power than prayer.

Family prayer does not have to be ritualistic, though it is wise to have times of scheduled prayer throughout the day or week. Prayer for each other should be woven into our daily routine. You set the table, and pray that your family will be fed with the bread of life, as well as natural food. When you see your husband getting dressed in the morning, pray, "God, clothe him with your garment of salvation and your robe of righteousness." When you send your kids off to school, pray that they will be a light that dispels darkness wherever they go.

It is true that, "a family who prays together stays together." There is no better first step.

- **NUMBER TWO: STIR UP THE GIFT OF GOD THAT IS IN YOU.**

The successful Christian home is one where each person can develop his or her special gifts. Romans 12 talks about personality gifts. For a complete guide to "personality gifts," please get a copy of my book, *Gifts That Shape Your Life and Change Your World.* Here are just three of the categories of different personalities:

- Prophet. These are passionate, emphatic, and black-and-white people. With them it's "my way or no way." They like things clear cut, and there is no middle ground.

- Teacher. These are more analytical people. They love accuracy and precision. They may seem colder, but their passion lies in their love of logic and learning.

- Merciful personality. These want everyone to love and forgive each other. Nothing matters to them as much as this.

I attended a seminar to learn to be more socially adept. I am goal-oriented and project-oriented. I feel that we are in a race, running a course, and we have to finish. As a result, I can sometimes hurt people's feelings on the way. So I wanted to be educated in fine-tuning my personality. I learned a lot about letting people be who they are.

All the prophets in the Bible had different personalities. Elijah was a director. He was socially awkward, but he got things done. Elisha was more relational. Paul was a director "Do this, do that. Achieve, run, press forward."

Luke was an analyzer, the last to write a Gospel. He had to do all the research before he was satisfied. Luke was the kind of guy who wanted all the pews lined up perfectly.

God gives everybody in a family different personalities, and the home should be a place where these personalities can develop safely. In my home, my wife Mary Jo likes working out the details and I am more of a big-picture director. I like to make big decisions but leave the small ones to other people. When she decorated the house, I didn't care to be involved in choosing the specific colors and decorations.

God gives everybody in a family different personalities, and the home should be a place where these personalities can develop safely.

Mary Jo is also very relational. She loves being with groups of people.

Not me. I love people like crazy, but I don't thrive on personal relationships as much as she does. In church I am friendly and social, but when I am with just one person I am socially awkward. I do not know what to say. As a result I tend to be self-contained. Give me a Bible and a place to pray or some task to do and I am happy all by myself.

Imagine taking those two different personality types on vacation. The husband is more self-contained than the socializer, so he arrives in Hawaii for their dream vacation and immediately stakes out a position on the bed, turns on the television and gets wrapped up in a golf game. The socializer says, "How can you watch television at a time like this? We are in Hawaii. We need to be taking helicopter rides, visiting pineapple plantations, going to a luau."

The husband thinks, "I thought this was a vacation. I want to relax."

I have learned that each personality in a family is a gift from God, put there intentionally. The home should be a place where these personality gifts can develop without fear of mockery. The successful Christian home should be a safe place. Paul wrote, "for God has not given us a spirit of fear; but of power, and love, and of a sound mind." The word "sound" means safe. Safe for your mind, safe for your emotions; a place where you are protected and can flourish just as God created you.

A married couple, who at one time attended our School of Pacesetting Leadership, sent me a beautiful letter. They said that for a long time, the joy of salvation had been missing from their home. After taking a class about discovering your ministry and gifts, they realized they could be used by God. Since then their joy has returned. Discovering their spiritual gifts led to a healthier home.

The home is supposed to be the primary Bible training institute. We often relegate our kids' spiritual training to Sunday school, children's church, and Christian schools and expect them to be raised in the faith by others. But God has called the family to be a microcosm of the Church. Children should learn how to get to Heaven, how to love God, how to do things properly and follow the principles of Jesus in the home, first. Sunday school, Christian school, and church activities should simply reinforce it.

Mary Jo and I were reading a book by Steve Bach. Steve did not have a safe home because his dad was a drunk. His book, called, *I Found Life Through Suicide*, was not based on his own experience, but his dad's. His dad would come home drunk and be violent and angry. Sometimes he would beat Steve's mother and the kids never knew what he would do next. But they loved and respected him and always feared that Mom might leave him. She stuck with him and told the kids, "Your dad is a good man. The war has upset his mind. We are going to pray it through."

It is important to let kids know that nothing is wrong with them.

Though she did not have the benefit of a Christian husband, she raised her kids in the admonition of the Lord and made their home as safe as she could. As a result, Steve went to Bible school and now ministers all over the country.

It is important to let kids know that nothing is wrong with them. God made them just the way they are. Even when a child's behavior is aberrant, we should never say things like, "What is wrong with you?" The problem is never personality but behavior, and there is a big difference between the two.

A successful Christian home should be a safe haven for children to get to know themselves, their personality traits and quirks — a place for them to understand themselves in the light of God's call on their lives.

- **NUMBER THREE: DO NOT OVERPROTECT YOUR CHILDREN OR YOUR SPOUSE.**

Husband, do not overprotect your wife. Wife, do not smother your husband. Sometimes people need a little space. Just because he wants to get out of the house and knock around some golf balls does not mean he is not committed to the family. Just because she wants to go to the mall does not mean she does not love you.

Even children need space away from their parents. When we fence our children in, we provide no opportunity for growth and they develop strange, antisocial behavior. It is particularly bad when parents overprotect their children in an effort to teach them biblical morality. Yes, we need to teach them to depend on the Bible, but we cannot force them to depend on it. If you try to make every decision for a child, he or she will become emotionally crippled and will not develop a sincere and faith-based relationship with God.

When my daughter was in high school, she wanted to attend the prom, but that conflicted with my commitment to discourage dancing. The denomination I belong to strongly opposes dancing, so when Trina said she wanted to attend the prom, I was on the horns of a dilemma. I could have been a dictator about it and said she was absolutely *not* going to the prom. But I concluded that she was mature enough to make her own decision. I could have forced her to stay home, but it would have taught her nothing and probably would have planted a seed of rebellion in her heart.

I let her make the decision and she went to the prom. Does that make her an irresponsible young lady? Not in the least. I believe it taught her to consider her decisions carefully and wisely. Her life today bears that out.

• NUMBER FOUR: DO NOT SHOW FAVORITISM.

Jacob favored his son Joseph and gave him more than he gave his other children. Finally, the other brothers were so jealous they threw Joseph in a pit. They then sold him to the slave-traders and told Jacob that a wild animal had killed him.

It happened in the previous generation too. Isaac favored Esau over Jacob because Esau was a tough guy. Rebecca favored Jacob. The brothers had relational problems with each other, even though they were twins.

Do not breed unnecessary problems between children or poison their relationships by letting them think you love one more than another. This falls into the same category of making your home a safe place. When you show favoritism it sends a clear signal that one kind of person or personality is favorable to another. Celebrate each of your children for who they are.

- **NUMBER FIVE: NEVER PUSH YOUR CHILD TO ACHIEVE, ESPECIALLY IF HE OR SHE IS NOT CAPABLE OF ACHIEVING SOMETHING.**

I remember a young boy who developed a serious and painful disease that the doctor diagnosed as being caused by a nervous disorder. That boy confided in me and said, "My dad always wanted me to play football and I hated football. I would have rather been in the library reading a book." His dad told him, "I played football when I was your age. Your older brother played football. Real men play football." He felt great pressure from his dad to perform at something he was not capable of, and it led to a painful physical illness.

> *Celebrate each of your children for who they are.*

This is another manifestation of the "You're not good enough" message. If we are not careful, we can set up standards that are impossible to achieve, sending a signal to our kids that they are less than what we want them to be.

In a healthy home, children will gravitate to what they are good at and excel at it within the context of a loving environment.

- **NUMBER SIX: ALLOW EVERYBODY IN THE FAMILY TO BE CHILDISH AT TIMES.**

This one is far too often overlooked. Christians think they can't be silly because they are supposed to have their minds on heavenly things.

Hogwash! Everybody (kids *and* adults) need to goof off sometimes. It's normal and healthy. We need times of casting off conventional restraints and just *playing*.

My daughter Trina and I were home together while my wife Mary Jo and son David were out running errands. Trina and I found David's dirt bike in the garage. It had not been ridden all winter, so we decided to give it a go. Trina pushed me down the road to jump-start it, and when we finally got it going she hopped on the back and away we went.

If we are not careful, we can set up standards that are impossible to achieve.

We had so much fun! We went to a big lot with dirt mounds and rode all over them. Then we saw little kids and pretended to show them our tattoos.

All of a sudden we saw a car go by that looked like Mary Jo's. We were caught! We found a path through the woods, rode into a muddy creek, and plowed into a corn field. I had on brand-new white tennis shoes, and every time we got stuck and fell over they sloshed in the mud.

It started getting dark and we couldn't find our way out of the woods. It didn't help that there was no headlight on the bike. We came to somebody's back yard, and Trina said, "This is our only way out." I said, "We can't go through their yard." She said, "I don't know about you, but I'm going," and she hopped off the bike and walked through the yard to the road. Then she whispered, "Dad, it's all clear, come on," so I rode the bike through real fast, right over the curb and onto the street. "Hop on," I said, "let's get out of here."

Make sure every member of your family is going to Heaven.

What if people had seen me riding around on a dirt bike? Who cares? Pastors are people too. We can't pretend we're above all that or we'll go crazy.

If someone in your family starts acting silly, don't ask what is wrong with him or her. Let your kids play in the mud. Join in with them once in a while. Go to a roller coaster park and ride the wildest rides. Go to a go-cart track and race each other.

Do whatever gets you out of a predictable mind-set and it will be like a fresh wind blowing through your household.

- **NUMBER SEVEN: MAKE SURE EVERY MEMBER OF YOUR FAMILY IS GOING TO HEAVEN.**

This is the most important issue in any family. A family related by blood needs to make sure they are also brothers and sisters in the family of God, partaking of the same Spirit. When that happens, a family becomes virtually unstoppable.

A scary thing happened to me one year when our church was presenting the *Passion Play*. I was in my office praying and looking through the window. I saw people going into the sanctuary to get their seats. I also saw my wife and children walking by. They could not see or hear me, but I was excited to see them. Then, I thought, "what if I was in Heaven and they were going into hell and there was nothing I could do to reach them?" The frustration would be more than I could bear.

I don't want any father, mother, or child to experience that frustration. There are plenty of opportunities to talk with your child about Christ, and perhaps you will even have the pleasure of leading him or her to the Lord.

Cultivating a successful home will help your church in ways you may never know. You will be happier, the church will be healthier, and your ministry will thrive.

In the next chapter we will move into a discussion of spiritual warfare and what it means to enforce Christ's victory.

SUCCESS POINTS:

1. Are there areas in your family life that need improvement? What are they?

2. How does a healthy family help a church?

God intends for churches to fight those principalities and powers together and take entire cities for His glory.

CHAPTER

ENFORCING
CHRIST'S VICTORY

I picked up a newsletter recently and read an interesting story. A man was driving down the road and saw a limousine pulled over to the side with a flat tire. Such a sight might cause some people to think, "They can take care of themselves," or "It must be a drug lord. If I stop I might get shot." But this particular man decided to stop and give the limousine driver a hand.

Together, they changed the tire, and when they were done, the back window rolled down and the man inside said, "Thank you for stopping and helping us. I really appreciate it. Is there anything I can do for you?" The man started to refuse, then said, "Well, Valentine's Day is coming up. I think it would be neat if you sent my wife a dozen roses." The man in the limousine took his address, and on Valentine's Day, a dozen beautiful roses arrived in a black-tie box. Attached was a little note that said, "Happy Valentine's Day, and please tell your husband thanks again for helping us on the road. Signed, Donald Trump. P.S. I paid off your mortgage too."

Who knows what surprises await us when we step out of the norm!

We need to take chances like that. We need to be actively helpful, and aggressively kind. That leads us to the next thing you can do to help your pastor succeed.

ENFORCE CHRIST'S VICTORY OVER THE DEVIL

What do I mean by this? I mean that Jesus won a great victory over the enemy. He said:

> ...All power is given unto me in heaven and in earth.
> —Matthew 28:18b

Then He turned around and said to the Church:

> Go ye therefore, and teach all nations, baptizing them in the name of the Father, and of the Son, and of the Holy Ghost: Teaching them to observe all things whatsoever I have commanded you: and, lo, I am with you alway, *even* unto the end of the world. Amen.
> —Matthew 28:19-20

He invited us to be part of that victory. More than that, He commands us to carry out that victory.

When we were born again, we were not only born into God's family, we were commissioned into God's army. God's family is a place of comfort and grace; His army is a place of warfare and strain.

> Thou therefore, my son, be strong in the grace that is in Christ Jesus...Thou therefore endure hardness, as a good

> soldier of Jesus Christ. No man that warreth entangleth himself with the affairs of *this* life; that he may please him who hath chosen him to be a soldier.
>
> —2 Timothy 2:1, 3-4

As a Christian, you are no longer a civilian but a military enforcer of Christ's victory. We are lieutenants, captains, majors, and colonels. We are not passively floating through life but are in a constant state of expectation — anticipating the challenges we might meet on the battlefield of life.

As a Christian, you are no longer a civilian, but a military enforcer of Christ's victory.

If the people of a church want to enjoy God's grace without joining the battle, the church will be a pleasant but ineffective place. But when a church is full of battle-ready believers, nothing can stand in its way.

A CHURCH OF ENFORCERS

Hector Gimenez was a gangster in Buenos Aires, Argentina. He dealt drugs and was into money, magic, and power. One day he heard an evangelist preach about the power of Christ, and he accepted Jesus and began reading the Bible. Not only that, he *believed* everything he read in the Bible. Then Jesus said, "Hector, I want you to start a church in Buenos Aires. There are churches here already, but you are a man who will enforce My victory over the devil."

Hector began to pray, and God revealed to him some of the principalities, powers, and demonic strongholds in certain neighborhoods and cities. This is what Paul spoke of in Ephesians 6:12. Hector cast them down, in the Name of Jesus, and held evangelistic meetings where whole neighborhoods came to Christ.

Today his church has 80,000 members and holds nine services a day, seven days a week. They have a 150-foot tent called the Spiritual Intensive Care Unit for people who need deliverance and healing.

Hector enforces Christ's victory over the devil and so do the people in his church. Every day of our lives we have the same kind of opportunity. If we don't take it, the devil will roam freely and have his way with people.

The devil sometimes reminds me of a cat. If you have ever seen a cat catch a bird, you know what I mean. Somebody jokingly told me that he believed all cats were demon-possessed. I disagree, because I had two cats that were not demon-possessed. They were saved. The Bible says to preach the Gospel to every creature (Mark 16:15), and I did. But I cannot stand to watch cats torment a bird or mouse. A scratch here, a swat there, a broken leg, and after torturing the victim, mercilessly kills them. It is cruel and seems to serve no purpose other than to fulfill the cat's playfulness.

That is what the devil does. He lies in wait to pounce on a sheep, then tears it apart a little bit at a time, and finally does it in. That is his nature, his business.

FROM PULPIT TO PARK BENCH

A. A. Allen was a powerful minister in the 1950s. Many people were saved and healed and wondrous things happened in his ministry. One night a 350-pound woman came to a service and said the doctor told her to lose weight or she would die; it was putting too much strain on her heart. He prayed for her, and she deflated by about 200 pounds right in front of everyone.

But the media and Allen's fellow Christians started attacking him, and he took the attacks to heart and became withdrawn. He hid in fear of being hurt. Pretty soon he was lashing out at people and they would lash out at him, and the hurt grew.

While in Florida one time, he allegedly gave in to the temptation to buy some liquor. He remained in the ministry, but now he was drinking. He finally lost his ministry and ended up wandering the streets. People who saw him in that condition said he was unrecognizable.

The devil had batted him around, swatted him down, and then went in for the kill. The once powerful, beloved evangelist died alone and penniless.

HAND-TO-HAND COMBAT

We can keep that from happening to us. But before we can do corporate warfare, we must learn to handle our own weapons and defend ourselves and our families from attack.

How do you enforce Christ's victory over the devil in your life? God's Word says:

> Submit yourselves therefore to God. Resist the devil, and he will flee from you.
> —James 4:7

We resist the devil the same way Jesus did, with the sword of the Spirit, which is the spoken Word of God. This does not mean carrying a physical Bible with us the way some people carry guns. The physical Bible is not powerful, but the words within it are. When the Word of God becomes part of us and we speak it from a believing heart, there is nothing in the universe as powerful.

> *We resist the devil the same way Jesus did, with the sword of the Spirit, which is the spoken Word of God.*

When Jesus and the disciples traveled by boat to the other side of the Sea of Galilee, a storm came up. Most people believe storms are natural phenomena and cannot be prayed against. But Jesus spoke to the storm, and the winds died down; the sea smoothed out. If you talk to the wind, people might think you are crazy, but Jesus did it. He even spoke to trees! (Matthew 21:19). I am convinced the devil brought that storm to stop them, but Jesus used it to teach them how to fight the forces of darkness. How do you fight these forces?

You speak *to* the problem and tell it to go, in Jesus' Name! The disciples spoke *about* the storm with no effect. But Jesus spoke *to* the storm, "Be still!" And the storm obeyed. That is a template for how we are to do battle on an individual level.

EXPECT GOD TO DO SOMETHING

When I discovered the power and authority we have in Jesus' Name, I began living in a state of heightened expectation, and so did our church. Not only did we expect to hear from God when we gathered together, we expected Him to deliver people from demons, fill people with the Holy Ghost, and heal and save to the uttermost.

But it began with small, seemingly unimportant things. One of the toilets in my home used to back up every other time we flushed, and I got tired of cleaning it up. I had read an old, hardback book by T. L. Osborn about the authority we have in Jesus Christ. And there I was, looking at the toilet backing up again. So I decided to try it out. I said, "In the Name of Jesus, go down and not up." The water went right down and I felt full of faith, even though my problem had only been a stopped-up toilet!

The knowledge and wisdom of our authority in Christ permeated the rest of my life too. I preached a series about it at my church. One man was so excited that when he went outside and saw bees buzzing under the canopy, he said, "I command you to go, in the Name of Jesus." The bees flew off and he ran back in and said, "It really works, Pastor Dave!"

Those are small things, but they illustrate the approach we must have to win individual skirmishes with the devil. Those small battles prepare us for the larger battles that, as a church, we fight in the spiritual realm. If we are not fighting and winning in our everyday life, how can we expect to come together as a church and enforce Christ's victory?

God intends for churches to fight those principalities and powers, together and to take entire cities for His glory. That is what the next chapter is about.

SUCCESS POINTS:

1. How do you personally enforce Christ's victory over the devil on a day-to-day basis?

2. Are there areas in your life that require more "enforcement"?

Spiritual warfare is simply enforcing the victory Christ won for us on the Cross.

ENGAGING
IN SPIRITUAL
WARFARE

In the last chapter we learned about enforcing Christ's victory on a personal level. Now we are going to learn about enforcing Christ's victory on a corporate level. The first-century church did this during a time of persecution. They had just been ordered by the religious hierarchy not to teach or preach in the Name of Jesus, so they came together and interceded corporately:

> And when they heard that, they lifted up their voice to God with one accord, and said, Lord, thou *art* God, which hast made heaven, and earth, and the sea, and all that in them is: Who by the mouth of thy servant David hast said, Why did the heathen rage, and the people imagine vain things? The kings of the earth stood up, and the rulers were gathered together against the Lord, and against his Christ.

> For of a truth against thy holy child Jesus, whom thou hast anointed, both Herod, and Pontius Pilate, with the Gentiles, and the people of Israel, were gathered together, For to do whatsoever thy hand and thy counsel determined before to be done. And now, Lord, behold their threatenings: and grant unto thy servants, that with all boldness they may speak thy word, By stretching forth thine hand to heal; and that signs and wonders may be done by the name of thy holy child Jesus. And when they had prayed, the place was shaken where they were assembled together; and they were all filled with the Holy Ghost, and they spake the word of God with boldness.
>
> —Acts 4:24-31

The religion that purported to worship God but which, according to Jesus, was satanically controlled, was telling the true Church not to preach or teach in the Name of Jesus. The Church went to battle to enforce Christ's victory so that:

• they would speak the Word with boldness.

• the sick would be healed.

• signs and wonders would follow them.

This is an example of ground-level warfare, dealing with demons that are low in the hierarchy, probably comparable to privates or corporals in the U.S. Army. Fighting them is like fighting in the trenches. Jesus did it all the time when he cast demons out of people. This level of demon harasses the church, tries to put up obstacles to the Gospel, and makes people physically or mentally ill.

I have dealt with this kind of demon before. At times I have prayed for people who felt they could not accept Christ for some reason. They said it was as if something was holding them back. When I started praying for them they let out a violent noise as if from their belly, and, instantly, they were set free and able to accept Jesus Christ. That is ground-level warfare.

These kinds of demons also go from one generation to another, using the same temptations or vices to enslave people. I remember a mother who was at the funeral of her daughter, who had committed suicide, and the mother kept saying, "I can't understand why she did it." And yet, the mother had attempted suicide twice, and there was a long history of suicide in the family.

Was it simply emotional distress or mental problems? No, I believe an evil spirit went from generation to generation tempting them with suicide. Different families have different problems, but until someone stands up and resists it, in Jesus' Name, that problem will persist.

HIGHER LEVELS, BIGGER DEVILS

There is a second level of warfare that involves religions: the occult and satanism. This level seems to be a little more intense and the evil spirits more powerful. This is not the kind of warfare you can fight on your own. You want a group of powerful believers praying together.

I have faced this kind of warfare. When people from certain Satanic religions found out I was coming to their city, they tried to disrupt the meetings. One witch coven had sent a witch into the service, and she began to cast spells on the service. We felt the oppression in that service, but Jesus won out because the witch heard the Gospel and decided to accept Jesus and leave the coven.

Then there is a third level of warfare, which Dr. C. Peter Wagner, a man who has studied spiritual warfare for many years, calls the strategic level. The generals and officers in Satan's army are at this level, and they are powerful. They gain strongholds over families, businesses, neighborhoods, cities, tribes, cultures and nations. They put roots down in a city and guard it like a junkyard dog.

Have you ever driven from one city to another and felt the difference in the spiritual atmosphere? I am a private pilot, and sometimes I take friends or family to other cities for a cup of coffee and to enjoy the sights. The minute the plane lands, I sense either the oppression or the liberty in that town, and usually the people with me do as well.

If you visit a city full of praying people, the whole atmosphere is entirely different. You feel invigorated and refreshed just being there.

Several years ago a group of Christians went to Guatemala and began to fast and pray and cast down evil principalities. When they preached the Gospel, tens of thousands of people came to Christ. Today 30 percent of the population in Guatemala claims to be born again and Spirit-filled.

A few hundred miles north of Guatemala is Guadalajara, Mexico, a city of six million people. There are only 160 churches in the whole city and nearly all of them have fewer than 100 people. Why? Because Satan has set up a stronghold and is keeping people from hearing — really hearing — the Gospel.

IDENTIFYING STRONGHOLDS

How can we know if there is a stronghold in our city? Our family? Our church? Here is a basic principle I have learned:

We know the devil has set up a stronghold when situations or circumstances do not make sense.

The devil creates misery and confusion and influences people to act irrationally. A man commits adultery when his wife is much more beautiful than the new lover. A family prays for revival, and when it comes, they leave the church. A wife prays for her husband to get saved, and when he does, she stops going to church.

I have seen each of these things happen, and each situation has Satan's fingerprints all over it.

We know the devil has set up a stronghold when situations or circumstances do not make sense.

We know he is at work when nothing else makes sense. When we have tried wars on poverty, poverty has escalated; when we have invested billions of dollars in the drug war, the drug situation has grown worse; when we have taxed and spent on social programs, things have not improved. It is not a political, social, or economic problem, it is a spiritual problem. Until we deal with the root, we will have no success.

The same is true in churches. If there is strife in your church and it seems to come from nowhere, you had better believe the devil has something to do with it. He comes in and creates division out of nothing. Quarrels seem to appear out of thin air and arguments have no rational basis. That is the devil's signature.

A MONSTER IN LANSING

In the 1980s our church broke ground for a massive building program. I learned about spiritual warfare right in the middle of it. I had never heard about spiritual warfare and there were few, if any, books or tape series about it at the time. And yet I was under tremendous spiritual attack and did not know from one day to the next if I was going to make it through.

We broke ground and decided, under the direction of the Lord, not to lay a single brick until we had a million dollars in cash and a buyer for our old building. I had fasted three days and God said, "Do not go to the bank and borrow money. If you do, the hip socket of Mount Hope Church is going to be knocked out, and you are going to wobble to and fro like a drunkard. I will never again lift you to the greatness I have brought you to today."

I went to the church board and told them this, not knowing that some had already gone behind my back and tried to get a bank to loan the church money. Board members started coming to my office saying they were going to withhold their tithes because they did not believe in what I was doing. They said we had to borrow money or we were going to be the laughingstock of the community.

They snuck off to the bank to try to get the money, began to excavate the land, and pour the foundation. When I found out about it I stopped it immediately, but by that time the church was in a dire crisis.

That's when I discovered what it is like to face the most powerful demonic forces I have ever known. I felt all alone, like not one person understood what I was facing. I was tormented on the inside. Every day there was a new rumor about me. I would find corporate documents tampered with. I discovered I was getting a different copy of the board minutes than the board was getting. I found corruption all over the church. I didn't know what to do about it.

My kids came home and asked, "Dad, why are you a liar? We learned in junior church that you are a liar." My attitude became horribly negative. Darkness was all around me, and I did not know who to turn to, because I didn't always know who my friends were.

A friend whom I did trust went to Chicago with me for a meeting. Back home the new church building had stopped and weeds were growing up on the new property. There was little hope in my heart that it would ever be built.

But something happened in Chicago that had never happened to me before. I was in bed at 10:32 p.m. My roommate was in the shower. I didn't know if I was going crazy or if the stress had finally gotten to me. I was praying in the Spirit as best I could, because I didn't know exactly how to pray anymore.

In that moment, I either fell asleep or God gave me a vision. I was hovering northeast of the church building we were worshipping in at the time, and I looked up and saw the most hideous creature over Lansing I have ever seen in my life. He was mean, evil, and violent; and in his right hand he had a curved sword. In his left hand he held a huge net with tens of thousands of people who were writhing around like fish in a net. Some were trying to find a way out. Others did not even know they were in the net. I felt so sorry for those people, and I knew intuitively that this creature was some kind of a principality or power over Lansing. It was holding people captive, tormenting their lives day in and day out. He wanted them all to go to hell but not before torturing them with tragedy, pain, disease, and calamity.

I said to the creature, "Let those people go," and he acted like, "Who are you, runt?" He shook his head and held them all the tighter. I repeated my command and he shook his head and held them tighter, making his victims suffer even more.

Then I looked down into the church — I could see through the roof. I was in the pulpit with my hands up, and I was teaching the people to put their hands up, but this was not worship. This was the church united, doing warfare against that satanic principality on behalf of the people held in his miserable net. We were all pointing to the northeast where I had seen this principality, and we were saying, "In the Name of Jesus, we command you, by His shed blood, to loose those people." He would shake his head and get violently angry, holding them all the tighter.

Like a battering ram, we did it again and again until, finally, we loosened his grip. I saw little pieces of the net began to break, as if invisible angels with scissors were cutting it apart. People began falling out, and they fell right into Mount Hope Church, where they wandered around looking confused. I knew we had to take care of those people.

Suddenly I was back in my hotel room thinking, "Wow, that was a weird dream." I like to write experiences, blessings, or miracles down; so I wrote down, "10:32 p.m., Chicago, principality," just to remind myself of the experience the next morning.

As it turned out, I didn't need anything to remind me. I lay back on the bed, praying in the Spirit, feeling sorry for myself, because it seemed like everybody back home was against me. I said, "God, I have only tried to obey you," and so on, with my griping. Suddenly, I found myself in a delivery room at a hospital. There was a woman on the table. I somehow knew she represented Mount Hope Church and I was her birthing coach. I was saying, "Push, push, push." Her face was red and sweaty, her neck veins popping out from so much labor, but she was very aloof toward me — not friendly. Every mother knows that when you are in labor, you do not feel very jovial.

I could see the head of the baby emerging. I kept saying, "Push harder." The head came out, then the shoulders, and then the whole body. The nurse picked up the baby and wrapped him in the blanket. The mother relaxed and got a beautiful smile on her face. But it wasn't over. I looked, and another baby came out. I thought, "Twins." Then another baby came out, and then dozens more. This woman was a baby-producing machine! As soon as a nurse picked one up, another one would come out.

Then I found myself suddenly back in my hotel room, and it was still 10:32 p.m. Not even a few seconds had gone by, but it seemed as though I was in that delivery room for 20 minutes or more.

Now I *knew* I was cracking up. I lay down again, still praying in the Spirit, wondering if I would survive the church crisis, and another vision came to me. This time, I was flying through the air from Chicago to Lansing. I could feel the breeze on my face. In a matter of seconds I was over Lansing, where a force stopped me and lowered me to the corner of our new church property. I knew what was there: A half-built foundation, unsightly weeds, and an ugly sign that read, "Future Home of Mount Hope Church."

> *I knew it was the voice of God. It was so loving and peaceful.*

I was humiliated and in such a state of mind that I no longer cared if it ever got built. Then I heard a tender, deep voice say, "David, look what I am doing." I knew it was the voice of God. It was so loving and peaceful. I folded my arms and said, "No, Lord, I am not going to look. I obeyed you. I didn't go to the bank and borrow money. Now my reputation is practically ruined. I am the laughingstock of the city. Friends have turned against me. I think I have become the gossip piece of the world."

I heard it again. "David, look what I am doing." I heard a truck coming down the road, shifting its gears. I didn't know if I was standing in the street or up on the sidewalk. So I looked at the truck and it was carrying all kinds of building materials. It turned onto the property. I turned and looked and, behold, there was our church building, three quarters of the way finished. I saw the towers, the structure, with plastic hanging over the entrances. I distinctly saw bags of concrete with plastic over them and bricks holding the plastic down. I was in awe. I realized that *God* was going to build this church. It was not going to be merely a *human* effort.

Just that quickly, I was back in my hotel room. My roommate, also named Dave, was still in the shower. I looked at my watch. It was still 10:32 p.m.

SHARING THE VISION

I did not want to tell anybody, but the next day on the way home, I was compelled to tell Dave. As I related it to him, his eyes became like saucers. He whispered reverently, "Dave, that was God."

I decided to share it with the church on Sunday, and afterward, we went into 21 days of warfare, as Daniel had done. I asked the staff to come in at 6 a.m. and we would pray until 9 a.m. God began revealing things about our church that I had never known. We began to identify controlling spirits, manipulating spirits, and rebellious spirits. We began to realize that Satan had a stronghold in our church, that he had tried to run the church by manipulation, control, and rebellion. Without realizing what we were doing (because we had no teaching on warfare then), we started binding unwanted spirits and casting them out.

Within weeks, 100 people wanted out of the church. I sat in my office, crying as I signed their membership transfers and said, "Lord, the church is falling apart," and He said, "Just let me do what I am doing."

The weeks that followed were difficult, but when I looked at the attendance numbers I realized there was no dip, even though 100 people had left. In fact, the church was growing. The offering went up by $10,000 a week. It was a miracle.

When I gave altar calls, three times as many people would come to Christ than in the past. It was like babies being born every week. Before, 10 or 12 people would come to Jesus at one altar call, but now, 30 or 40 people were coming every week. Other miracles occurred. A deaf lady came up after the service and said God had restored her hearing.

Shortly thereafter, the church accountant ran to my office and announced to me, "We have our million dollars. We can start building." I said, "Where did that come from?" I thought the building program had stalled, but God had been working to bring it to pass. People had donated houses they could not sell. The church put them on the market and they sold immediately. People gave valuables to the church with no suggestion or coaxing from me.

Then we hired an engineer to inspect the foundation that the former board members and their bunch had laid. He declared it to be faulty and dangerous. If we had built on it, it could have collapsed, killing the people inside the sanctuary. We couldn't believe our ears. The wrong concrete was used. We had two other independent engineers inspect the foundation. They both concurred; the foundation was unsafe and the excavation was done improperly.

God did not want us to start building because He wanted our building to be safe! We excavated, tore out the old foundation, laid the new foundation and the building started going up.

One day at a board meeting I suggested we go to the new property. The building was three quarters of the way up and we had not borrowed a penny. There was the plastic hanging over the entrances, just as I had seen in the vision. There were bags of cement with plastic over them and bricks on the corners. I had chills because I was seeing what I had already seen. I looked into the sky, and two circular rainbows appeared, hanging over the property as a sign of God's grace. For a while we stood staring at those two beautiful halo rainbows, and I knew God's favor was upon us.

I have come to the subject of spiritual warfare from a practical level. I have lived it. I have learned from it. I have not studied it as extensively as some Christians, but I know it is real, and I know our church has experienced significant breakthroughs when we have banded together to fast and pray. I believe that this type of spiritual warfare is critical if any church is to make inroads into its city or community.

When we enter any kind of warfare, we must enter from a position of victory. Spiritual warfare is simply enforcing the victory Christ won for us on the Cross. Even in very difficult situations such as the one I went through — and I know mine was not the worst — God will teach us to fight and beat the enemy as a church body empowered by the Holy Spirit.

With a group of battle-ready believers and the Lord working with you, your church can achieve the impossible!

SUCCESS POINTS

1. Can you think of a time you faced a disappointment that turned out later to be a blessing?

2. Make a list of what you'll do to be a vital part of your pastor's spiritual warfare.

When we properly handle
being "number two," a spiritual
law goes into effect, and
God honors us.

CHAPTER

TRUSTING GOD WHEN YOU ARE "NUMBER TWO"

In this chapter I want to discuss a problem I frequently encounter that requires a great deal of maturity, particularly for associate ministers and pastor's spouses.

Have you ever been the life of the party, but somebody came along who was funnier than you? Have you ever felt suddenly overshadowed? Humbled? Like you had become the second brightest star in the room?

Maybe you tried out for a leading role in the Christmas production, but the directors assigned you a lesser role.

Maybe you wanted to sing in the ladies' trio on Easter Sunday, but the choir director chose someone else, and you had to sing backup.

Maybe you applied for a position on the church staff, but somebody else got the job.

Maybe you wanted to help lead the missions trip, but the missions director did not feel you were ready yet.

Everybody knows the feeling of being "number two." All of us are number two in something. In fact, most of us probably spend our lives being "number two" (or three or four) in most areas. Learning what to do when you are "number two" will greatly help your church to function and will make you a better person.

FAMOUS "NUMBER TWO"

One of the most famous "number two's" in the Bible is John the Baptist. For a while he was the star of Israel, gathering all the crowds and receiving all the press. Hundreds, even thousands, came to hear him speak in the wilderness.

He had power. He had influence.

When he said to "repent and be baptized," people did. Israel was in the palm of his hand ...

... and then one day, out of the crowd, stepped Jesus.

John saw Jesus coming toward him and said, "Look, the Lamb of God, who takes away the sin of the world!"

"This is the one I meant when I said, 'A man who comes after me has surpassed me because he was before me.'"

"I myself did not know him, but the reason I came baptizing with water was that he might be revealed to Israel." Then John gave this testimony:

> And John bare record, saying, I saw the Spirit descending from heaven like a dove, and it abode upon him. And I knew him not: but he that sent me to baptize with water, the same said unto me, Upon whom thou shalt see the Spirit descending, and remaining on him, the same is he which baptizeth with the Holy Ghost. And I saw, and bare record that this is the Son of God. Again the next day after John stood, and two of his disciples; And looking upon Jesus as he walked, he saith, Behold the Lamb of God! And the two disciples heard him speak, and they followed Jesus.
>
> —John 1:32-37

Can you imagine experiencing such a drastic "demotion"? One day he was the talk of the town; the next he was checking into his room at the Herod Hotel.

One day he was speaking the words of God to Israel. The next, he was having to say, "Don't pay attention to me anymore. I'm not 'the man' — He is."

John could have tried to maintain his number-one status. He could have ignored Jesus. He could have joined the religious leaders in criticizing Him. But he didn't. Instead he used the influence God had given him to steer people to Jesus, thus spelling the end of his own ministry. He acknowledged that Jesus had to increase while he himself had to decrease. He watched his disciples walk away. He watched the crowds dwindle. He saw their fascination and attention switch over to this Man from Galilee who John knew was the Lamb of God.

Eventually, after being imprisoned by Herod, John was beheaded. So ended the earthly life of the man Jesus called "the greatest of the Old Testament prophets." In him we find a model of how to be "number two."

And you…?

What do you do when you are "number two?" Do you sulk, drag your feet, or talk against whoever is number one?

When I was at a minister's conference in Oklahoma, years ago. I sat next to a gentleman who introduced himself and said he was pastor of a church of 750 people in Illinois. He was older than me, and I didn't want to compare churches, so I told him I pastored a church up in Michigan, hoping that would end it. But I could tell by the look in his eye that he wanted to know the specifics, and finally he blurted out, "How many people are you running up there?" I'm sure He thought I was going to say 150 or 180. While I did not lie, I did estimate conservatively, and said we were running about 3,200 at the time.

The man did not talk to me the rest of the conference. He would not even acknowledge that I was sitting next to him. His pride had been pricked and he felt the sting of being "number two," at least in our row of seats.

I read an article by a man named Bob, who, when he was in high school, was dazzled by a particular girl named Doris. One day Doris walked up to him in the hall and said, "Hi, Bob," and he said, "Hi, Doris." The bell rang, so she said, "I better get to my next class," and she reached out, touched his right arm, and when she did, he tensed up. She said, "Wow, Bob, you have quite a muscle."

Bob felt emboldened by the compliment, so he said, "You ought to feel it when I flex it. In fact," he said, sucking in his stomach, "punch me in the stomach. It is made of steel." She declined, but he insisted, and by now his friends were standing around. She wound up and punched him in the stomach, pulled her hand back, and said, "That is solid." Bob, smiling weakly, said, "I told you," walked over to his locker, put his head inside, and threw up.

After that incident, he wrote, "I do not believe I have ever gained anything by trying to impress people. It is a game for losers, and the world can keep it."

What happens when somebody more impressive than you comes along? Somebody a little smarter? Somebody a little more attractive? Somebody who is better with numbers, words, music, babies, or people?

Maybe you have been the king of a certain department in the church and somebody comes along with more talent than you, and suddenly you find that you are "number two." Or, you have worked your way up in a company, and they hire a young man with an M.B.A. who is full of energy and fresh ideas that once were yours. You find that you are in the shadows and he is in the spotlight. What do you do?

LEARNING TO BE SECOND

I read a story about a student at the University of California in Berkeley, who was in the library studying. He noticed that other students in the library were studying too, and he started screaming and running through the library yelling, "Stop studying! You are getting ahead of me!"

A famous British Baptist preacher, E.B. Meyer, was a world-renowned preacher and wrote some wonderful books.

One time he went to a conference where G. Campbell Morgan was speaking. Morgan was drawing bigger crowds to his sessions than Meyer was and Meyer became jealous. He went home and prayed, "God, how can I overcome these feelings?" The Lord said the only way was to pray that God would bless Morgan even more.

Competitiveness can cause friction in marriages too. Sometimes a wife is very spiritual, goes to church often, and one day, her husband gives his life to Jesus and develops an insatiable desire to study God's Word. He starts growing by leaps and bounds beyond the wife, and suddenly, the wife finds herself as "number two" and she has a choice: Does she rejoice with him or does she resist him? Believe it or not, I have seen women leave the church and walk away from God in that kind of situation.

Back in the 1920s, there was a famous battle in New York city between Chrysler and Manhattan Bank and the competing architects designing their buildings. The architects at Manhattan Bank found out how tall the Chrysler building was going to be and they added a pole, 57 feet high, with a lantern on top — making the Manhattan Bank a little bit taller than the Chrysler building.

But the architects of the Chrysler building had another trick up their sleeves: they added a spire, 185 feet tall, that made the Chrysler building the tallest building in the world at that time.

It is best not to compete. We do well to learn this early. There is always going to be somebody ahead of you in some area of life.

Once we come to terms with this, we can rest and find blessings in being "number two." Number two's are blessed when they handle this position properly. They have an incredible opportunity to become mature Christians and to accomplish much for God, though they may not always get the credit from people.

Elisha was "number two." He tagged along behind Elijah, and people did not want to deal with him because Elijah was the "real prophet." But Elisha stayed faithful to Elijah, and in the end had twice the anointing of Elijah and performed twice the miracles. His reward was to be elevated to number one, but only after years of being "number two."

Being number two can be a blessed preparation for receiving a double or triple anointing.

Being "number two" can be a blessed preparation for receiving a double or triple anointing. Timothy was "number two," a timid young man with stomach problems. Paul always had to write to churches and tell them to receive Timothy as they would Paul himself. But history tells us that Timothy became the founder of the church growth movement. He became pastor of the Ephesian church that grew to over 30,000 souls.

Timothy, who was a "number two," ended up becoming number one. But first, he was faithful at being "number two."

When we handle being "number two" in a proper way, whether it is in the home, a business, or a ministry, God can give us twice as many blessings as the number one person had because He knows we will be faithful.

BEING A GREAT "NUMBER TWO"

How should we handle those times when we work in someone else's shadow? Follow these steps:

• NUMBER ONE: DO YOUR JOB WELL.

God said to Cain, "If you do well, will you not be accepted too?" If you are "number two" on the basketball team, do well as "number two." If the number one player makes more baskets and you are a better dribbler, dribble well, and pass when it is time to shoot. He will score the points, but the whole team will benefit.

• NUMBER TWO: POSITION YOURSELF AS "NUMBER TWO."

Don't try to convince people you are number one. Avis car rental company acknowledged that they were second to Hertz but turned it to their advantage and made their slogan, "We try harder."

Hendrik Himler was the Gestapo chief under Hitler. After Hitler was dead and World War II had ended the Allied investigators came looking for war criminals. Before they did Himler decided to disguise himself as an enlisted man in the army. He shaved his mustache and put a black patch over his eye, but refused to wear a private's uniform. He said, "If I am going to be an enlisted man, I want to have some authority," so he put on a sergeant's uniform.

When the Allied investigators came in, they ordered that all army personnel with a rank of sergeant or above be arrested, and that is how they caught Himler. If he had posed as a private he would have fled to freedom, but he was too proud to wear a private's uniform. He just could not be a "number two."

I have a friend who is a pastor in East Lansing. When our church in Lansing was growing so fast, he had a decision to make. He could bad-mouth us like some churches in town did, or he could go in a positive direction.

Do you know what he did? He positioned himself as "number two," started getting tapes of my preaching and told his congregation, "We are going to become on the east side of town like Mount Hope Church is on the west side." He honored me and my church, and as a result, now has one of the fastest growing churches in Michigan. If he continues to grow, he will far overshadow Mount Hope Church. I will then be "number two!" And I will rejoice in the young man's success.

• NUMBER THREE: PRAY FOR NUMBER ONE.

Stephen Covey wrote a book in which he said there are two kinds of people: those with an abundance mentality and those with a scarcity mentality. People with the scarcity mentality believe if someone else gets a bigger piece of the pie, their piece will automatically get smaller. People with an abundance mentality believe if someone else gets a big piece of the pie, the pie will grow and everybody will get a bigger piece.

I believe the Bible encourages an abundance mentality. After all, with God as our source, He can make the pie as big as He wants. That puts us in a position to cheer other people on even when it seems they are competing with us.

When we properly handle being "number two" a spiritual law goes into effect and God honors us. If you run a business and have a competitor across town, pray for that competitor to prosper because God will grow the pie, and you will get a bigger piece too. I see it happen all the time. If a person is jealous of number one, invariably their share of the pie shrinks, whether in business or ministry. But when "number two" prays for number one, spiritual abundance is released.

When Christians learn how to be "number two," a church can move forward much faster than if people drag their feet and feel resentment. As I said in the beginning of this book, now is not a time for dawdling. We are close to the return of Jesus. How miserable it would be on Judgment Day to realize that souls are missing from Heaven because we begrudged being "number two" and hindered someone's ministry!

But how wonderful to know that we served in the position where God put us, and that in the end all glory will go to Him alone.

SUCCESS POINTS

1. Can you list an area in which you are number one?

2. Can you list some people of various careers and professions that are number ones? Do you pray for their success?

W*hen you have a problem with someone in the church, go to him (or her) privately and discuss the matter.*

CHAPTER 10

PRACTICING LOVE AND WISDOM

PART 1

Pastor Frank stopped by the hospital to see Gladys, an elderly member of his congregation. They had a wonderful visit. Several others from the church visited Gladys that day, bringing her cheer and offering prayers.

The next day, Gladys' son, George, arrived to visit his mother. He asked, "Mom, has anyone from your church been here to see you?"

"No," she replied, "I've been all alone for two days now.

"What?" he shot back, "Are you telling me your pastor didn't even stop up to see you?"

"No," Gladys said, "Nobody's been here."

George grabbed the phone and called the church, demanding to know why the pastor hadn't come to the hospital to pray for his mother. He also complained about it to everyone that visited Gladys. "That pastor doesn't give a 'rip' about my mom." He was convincing every visitor, nurse and other medical people that his mother's church didn't care anything about her.

He affected the minds of dozens of people, based on what he believed to be true, but was, in fact, not the truth.

He didn't know that the pastor and several others from the church had been there for his mother, but because of her heavy medication, she didn't remember the visits.

When the pastor walked into the hospital room the next day, George wasn't there. Pastor Frank had a nice visit and a prayer with Gladys, and left the room when she fell asleep. When George returned he asked his mother if anyone had stopped to see her. She said, "No, I've been all alone all day."

Nobody knows the hazards of accepting the call as a pastor.

This happens more than you can imagine. And people believe the pastor doesn't care, that he's out on the golf course while his sheep suffer. Some church members seem to take a devilish delight in hurting their pastor, pointing out his shortcomings, rehearsing his faults, and even attacking his credibility.

Nobody knows the hazards of accepting the call as a pastor. Overwork, bellyaching members, knit-pickers, gossipers, and high-maintenance individuals take a terrible toll on the pastor's emotions, leaving him often fatigued and disenchanted. Is it any wonder that pastors stay an average of only three years in any one church? They hope their next parish – their next congregation – will be different.

FUELERS AND DRAINERS

But people are people. They're the same everywhere. You have in every church two basic categories of church members: (1) "Fuelers," those who enjoy the church, encourage the pastor, help out, get involved, and share the pastor's heart and vision. (2) "Drainers," those who try to suck the life out of almost everyone they meet, especially the pastor. Drainers are the high maintenance, dysfunctional members who seem to make it their business to drain the "fuel" out of any church leader they can corner.

In this chapter, I'm going to show you how to be a "fueler," and not a "drainer" for your pastor. I don't believe anyone wants to be known as a "drainer." Some are, but don't realize it. This chapter will show how you can help your pastor succeed by simply observing some practical issues you may not have thought about. It really all boils down to applying love and wisdom to every situation.

Love will put itself into another's shoes, in this case, your pastor's. Wisdom is the practical application of knowledge – ethics and etiquette, or "refined morality."

So here it is, a potpourri of practical love and wisdom for helping your pastor succeed.

1. PRAY FOR YOUR PASTOR AND HIS FAMILY DAILY.

This seems elementary, yet it's surprising how many members don't even mention their pastor in prayer even one day in any given week.

Two particular times your pastor needs special and intense intercession are the day before he ministers, and the day after. The day before he ministers is often a time when distractions come to divide his attention. The phone may ring non-stop, "drainers" may stop by to chat about nothing in particular, or the enemy may harass his family. On the day after he ministers, often depression will tempt him. If twenty people came to Christ, he'll wonder why it wasn't thirty. He'll recall all of his mistakes, feeling that he should have done better, or that more people ought to have been in church.

Pray for his and his family's protection. Use Psalm 91 as a guide, and as you pray, include your own family.

SPECIFIC THINGS TO PRAY FOR YOUR PASTOR[1]

- That he'll be blessed with a rich study time in preparation for ministry

- That he'll be shielded from the fear of man

- That he'll possess sound leadership wisdom

---

[1] Adapted from the following sources:

Jacobs, Cindy, *Possessing the Gates of the Enemy*, 1991, 1994 Chosen Books, Grand Rapids, MI 49516

Maxwell, John, *Partners in Prayer*, 1996, Thomas Nelson Publishers, Nashville, TN 37214

Teykl, Terry, *Your Pastor: Preyed On or Prayed For*, Prayer Point Press, Muncie, IN 47304

- That the Lord will anoint him with apostolic results: signs, wonders, miracles, and revelation

- That God will honor him with lasting fruit from his labors

- That God will cancel any satanic assignments against him

- That all obstacles to his ministry will be removed

- Rebuke all distractions from his devotional life

- Claim Scriptural promises of protection over him

- Bind any hindering and manipulating spirits in your pastor's life

- Loose the forces of Heaven to aid your pastor in prayer and ministry

- Give thanks for his calling and gifts

- Expect great things in the services led by your pastor

Yield to the Holy Spirit in other areas of intercession for your pastor.

2. DON'T ASK HIM TO INTERPRET YOUR DREAMS, VISIONS, OR MESSAGES YOU BELIEVE TO BE FROM THE LORD.

This sounds strange, I know. Yet practically every week someone wants their pastor to interpret a dream for them or some strange occurrence that happened to them. It's your job to interpret, not the pastor's. If you are not sure that something you are "hearing" or "seeing" is from the Lord, take the time to pray about it yourself.

You'd be amazed at how many dreams and visions the pastor has heard and how frustrating it is for him when people expect him to give the interpretation.

3. DON'T USE PRAYER MEETINGS, BANQUETS, OR SPECIAL MEETINGS AS YOUR OPPORTUNITY TO TAKE ADVANTAGE OF THE PASTOR'S ACCESSIBILITY.

Sometimes people will use these times to air their personal complaints with the pastor or try to set up an appointment with him rather than going through the channels he has established. There is an appropriate time, place, and approach to handling grievances and it's not the prayer meeting, the holy convocation, or the banquet. Remember, the pastor wants to enjoy a time of prayer at the prayer meeting too. He wants to enjoy being with people at the banquet. An ill-timed complaint can be draining during these special times.

4. BE RESPECTFUL OF HIS AND OTHER PEOPLE'S TIME.

After a service, I like to meet and greet as many people as I possibly can. I love people, and I love meeting new people. Unfortunately, at times, someone will talk to me non-stop while others are lining up, waiting to shake my hand or say a word to me. This happens to all pastors. People are waiting to greet him, but one person – and often the same person week-after-week – will be jabbering to the pastor about a recent vacation, new fishing boat, the football game, his most recent medical procedure – you name it. This is rude and unfair to others who would like to greet the pastor, and it puts a "monkey" on his back as he tries to pay attention to you, while seeing the others in his peripheral vision lining up.

5. KEEP GROWING SPIRITUALLY.

St. John said, "I have no greater joy than to hear that my children walk in truth." Walking implies moving – going somewhere. There is no greater joy for a pastor than to see the members growing spiritually.

Both the Apostle Paul and the Apostle Peter talk about spiritual growth, and both give some clues on how to identify those who are not growing.

> Wherefore laying aside all malice, and all guile, and hypocrisies, and envies, and all evil speakings, as newborn *babes,* desire the sincere milk of the word, that ye may grow thereby:
>
> –1 Peter 2:1-2
>
> And I, brethren, could not speak unto you as unto spiritual, but as unto carnal, *even* as unto babes in Christ. I have fed you with milk, and not with meat: for hitherto ye were not able *to bear it,* neither yet now are ye able. For ye are yet carnal: for whereas *there is* among you envying, and strife, and divisions, are ye not carnal, and walk as men?
>
> –Corinthians 3:1-3

Spiritual babies are carnally minded, typically acting with envy, whining about this or that. In my book, *Growing Up in Our Father's Family* [2], I give the reader the signs of spiritual babyhood.

Babies are always dependent upon others. Someone has to change them, feed them, and do things for them all the

---

2 Williams, Dave, *Growing Up in Our Father's Family*, 1982, Decapolis Publishing House, Lansing, MI 48917

time. Spiritual babies require constant attention and will be sure to behave in such a way as to get it.

Everything goes into a baby's mouth. My daughter would eat dirt, crayons, bugs, anything she could fit into her mouth. Spiritual babies are always taste-testing the new doctrines and fads that blow through town.

Babies are jealous. Spiritual babies wonder why someone else was selected for the leading role in the Easter play. They mutter words like this, "Why did the pastor visit Mr. Jones? He never visited me."

St. Paul also talked about spiritual children. They aren't babies but neither are they spiritually mature.

> That we *henceforth* be no more children, tossed to and fro, and carried about with every wind of doctrine, by the sleight of men, *and* cunning craftiness, whereby they lie in wait to deceive; but speaking the truth in love, may grow up into him in all things, which is the head, *even* Christ:
>
> –Ephesians 4:14-15

These verses speak of spiritual children as being unstable and having problems with their mouths.

Children are naturally curious, nosey, and snoopy. They always have their noses in someone else's business.

Children talk, talk, talk, talk, ad infinitum. A baby becomes a child when the nonstop talking begins. Spiritual children are usually jibber jabbering about something or someone.

Children are always trying to make an impression on someone. Spiritual children often say things like, "Look at this car the Lord gave me. It cost me $40,000, but it hauls my new boat just fine.

Children are know-it-alls.

Children have a habit of fighting with their brothers and sisters.

Children are unreliable.

Children are essentially undisciplined and unorganized in everyday practical matters.

Well, how does a believer grow up spiritually?

1. **Proper diet** – feast on the Word of God and good, solid teaching (1 Peter 2:2).

2. **Proper exercise** – exercise your faith, your service, your witness, your testimony. (Read Ephesians 4:14-16 in the Amplified Bible.)[3]

3. **Proper rest** – that is, resting in Jesus' finished work (Matthew 11:28; Hebrews 4:9-10).

It's an honor and a help to every pastor when church members are growing in Christ and in the faith. Maturing believers have less temptation to gripe, complain, criticize, and murmur. Maturing believers have less of a propensity to dwell on trials, magnify troubles, rehearse hurts, or hold grudges.[4]

---

3   Bible, The Amplified Version, 1954, 1958, 1962, 1964, 1965, 1987, The Lockman Foundation, La Habra, California

4   Finney, Charles, *Lectures on Revival of Religion*, Lecture 22, Growth in Grace, New York Evangelist Publications, 1835, New York, NY

No pastor wants an entire congregation of people wearing "fully loaded" spiritual diapers. To help your pastor succeed, make sure you are a growing disciple of Jesus Christ.

6. HANDLE YOUR CONFLICTS BIBLICALLY.

Don't bring your relational disagreements to the pastor, expecting him to solve them for you.

> Moreover if thy brother shall trespass against thee, go and tell him his fault between thee and him alone: if he shall hear thee, thou hast gained thy brother. But if he will not hear *thee, then* take with thee one or two more, that in the mouth of two or three witnesses every word may be established. And if he shall neglect to hear them, tell it unto the church: but if he neglect to hear the church, let him be unto thee as an heathen man and a publican.
>
> —Matthew 18:15-17

By simply obeying these words of our Lord, we would solve about 70% of all church problems. The plan is simple: When you have a problem with someone in the church, go to him (or her) privately and discuss the matter. Perhaps he doesn't even know he had offended you. If it doesn't get resolved in your private meeting, then take a second person with you when you talk to the offender. Only as a last resort are you to bring it to the church (probably by bringing it to the deacons or elders) for investigation and arbitration.

I was at a meeting in another church in town and spotted an old member of our church. I walked over to chat with him. He left our church years ago because someone in the media department said something that offended him. He never resolved it biblically, but simply walked out angry.

In our conversation, he told me he had been to four other churches since leaving ours.

"Yes, I went over to First Baptist for awhile, but the pastor didn't recognize all my gifts, so after about a year, I went over to the Brethren church. The pastor put me on staff there when he saw how good I was in music and technology. But after about a year and a half, I noticed the pastor had lost his vision, so I went over to Maranatha Church. But they weren't very spiritual there, so I came to the Assembly of God Church after a year or so. I've been here for nearly a year now, and I get to do all kinds of technological things I love doing. Yes sir, they really depend on me here. I don't know when God will move me on, though."

In the spirit realm, I could almost see a big spiritual diaper wrapped around this brother – containing a full load. If he only realized how immature he sounded. Until he learns to obey the words of Jesus in resolving conflicts, he'll drift and float, never growing up in God's family.

Handle conflicts the biblical way.

P*eople who gossip and murmur hurt the church, hurt the pastor, hurt productivity, and ultimately hurt themselves.*

11

PRACTICING LOVE AND WISDOM

PART 2

I realize I'm giving you these practical points on love and wisdom in a rapid-fire manner. Any one of them could be the subject of an entire book. But my intent is to give you bite-sized pieces so you can chew on them throughout the day, meditating on the principles and developing a personal plan on how you might be able to help your pastor succeed.

Okay. Let's continue …

7. AVOID SINS OF THE TONGUE AS IF THEY WERE A CONTAGIOUS DISEASE.

These sins are the kind that grieve the Holy Spirit and drain the anointing from the violators.

> Let no corrupt communication proceed out of your mouth, but that which is good to the use of edifying, that it may minister grace unto the hearers. And grieve not the Holy Spirit of God, whereby ye are sealed unto the day of redemption. Let all bitterness, and wrath, and anger, and clamour, and evil speaking, be put away from you, with all malice: and be ye kind one to another, tenderhearted, forgiving one another, even as God for Christ's sake hath forgiven you.
>
> —Ephesians 4:29-32

What is corrupt communication? Slander. Gossip. Backbiting. Griping. Murmuring. Rumor-spreading. Isn't it interesting that Christians cringe when they hear someone using curse words, yet they themselves often commit worse "crimes" against God using their tongues to gossip or to spread rumors, which ultimately hurt the church and the pastor?

> Behold, we put bits in the horses' mouths, that they may obey us; and we turn about their whole body. Behold also the ships, which though *they be* so great, and are driven of fierce winds, yet are they turned about with a very small helm, whithersoever the governor listeth. Even so the tongue is a little member, and boasteth great things. Behold, how great a matter a little fire kindleth! And the tongue *is* a fire, a world of iniquity: so is the tongue among our members, that it defileth the whole body, and setteth on fire the course of nature; and it is set on fire of hell.
>
> —James 3:3-6

TENSION IN THE CHURCH

Whenever there is tension in a church, someone is probably gossiping. Gossip is when you tell somebody something they don't need to know about somebody else. And the worst kind of gossip is when you "spiritualize" it by putting it into the form of a prayer request. "I'm only telling you this so you can pray more intelligently for Pastor Harold. Well, here's the scoop – and remember, I trust you with this information ..."

Oh - oh. I smell spiritual diapers again.

PROTECT YOUR PASTOR

Mary Ann was our pianist. One day somebody tried to give her a morsel of gossip, telling her some of the "problems with our church." Mary Ann pointed her finger at the person and firmly asserted, "Do my ears look like garbage cans? I don't need to hear that trash. I met Jesus in this church. I was filled with the Holy Spirit in this church. I know our pastor loves us in this church, and I'm not going to listen to your gossip. Period!" Needless to say, Mary Ann was deeply respected and nobody – I mean nobody – offered her any of their immature, wicked gossip ever again.

> *Murmuring brings disease to the heart and can bring devastating and disastrous consequences*

People who gossip and murmur hurt the church, hurt the pastor, hurt productivity, and ultimately hurt themselves.[5] The Bible says murmuring brings disease to the heart and can bring devastating and disastrous consequences.

---

5   Williams, Dave, *The Pastor's Minute*, p. 86 and 165, 2002, Decapolis Publishing House, Lansing, MI 48917

When someone tries to contaminate you with their murmuring gossip or gripes, you can stop them with these five questions:

1. *What's your reason for telling me this?*

2. *Where did you get your information?*

3. *Have you gone directly to the person?*

4. *Have you checked out your facts?*

5. *May I quote you when I check this out?*

When gossipers realize you're not going to allow your ears to become their garbage cans, they'll stop. And you'll have a good day, knowing you did something to protect your pastor instead of hurting him.

In Proverbs, it says there are six things the Lord hates, and the seventh is an abomination to Him. Number six is "a false witness that speaketh lies," and number seven is "he that soweth discord among brethren."[6] And meditate on these Scriptures:

> A good man's mind is filled with honest thoughts; an evil man's mind is crammed with lies. The wicked accuse; the godly defend. The wicked shall perish; the godly shall stand.
>
> —Proverbs 12:5-7 (TLB)
>
> Gentle words cause life and health; griping brings discouragement.
>
> —Proverbs 15:4 (TLB)

---

6   Proverbs 6:16-19

GET RID OF THE GOSSIP

Solomon said to get rid of the gossiper and tensions will disappear. Very few people understand the seriousness of the sin of gossip. Gossip separates friends. Gossip causes tension. When gossip stops, tensions in a church dissolve.

> Fire goes out for lack of fuel, and tensions disappear when gossip stops.
>
> —Proverbs 26:20 (TLB)

If gossip is such a hideous sin, why do gossipers continue? The Bible gives us a little insight in Proverbs where it says the gossiper has a wicked heart. That's one reason. Another reason may be that gossipers have such low self-esteem they think that talking about someone else will cause them to feel elevated in the eyes of others.

A gossiper is untrustworthy.

A gossiper is nobody's friend.

People who commit sins of the tongue usually associate with those who are guilty of the same sin. They enjoy the company of others who are like-minded.

> The wicked enjoy fellowship with others who are wicked; liars enjoy liars.
>
> —Proverbs 17:4 (TLB)

Gossip is named in the same list as murder.

> Their lives became full of every kind of wickedness and sin, of greed and hate, envy, murder, fighting, lying, bitterness, and gossip. They were backbiters, haters of God, insolent, proud, braggarts, always thinking of new ways of sinning and continually being disobedient to

their parents. They tried to misunderstand, broke their promises, and were heartless—without pity. They were fully aware of God's death penalty for these crimes, yet they went right ahead and did them anyway and encouraged others to do them, too.

—Romans 1:29-32 (TLB)

A person walking in the law of love does not gossip.

For all the law is fulfilled in one word, *even* in this; Thou shalt love thy neighbour as thyself. But if ye bite and devour one another, take heed that ye be not consumed one of another.

—Galatians 5:14-15

I think you get an idea of what God thinks about the sin of gossip, murmuring, and other sins of the tongue. If you really want to help your pastor succeed, be a builder with your words. Speak words of life and power over your church and pastor. Speak the Word of God over your pastor. Give him encouraging words. The brightest lights in our church are those who constantly speak encouraging words of faith to others; those who refuse to lose their anointing in mindless sins of the tongue.

Being number two can be a blessed preparation for receiving a double or triple anointing.

Here's a good practice: Replace all sins of the tongue with thanksgiving.

> In every thing give thanks: for this is the will of God in
> Christ Jesus concerning you. Quench not the Spirit.
>
> —1 Thessalonians 5:18-19

Do you want to be known or remembered as a busybody,
slander-mongering gossiper? Or do you prefer to be recognized as one who uses kind, gentle words to bless, encourage,
and provide a lift to people's day? It's your choice. The latter is a "fueler" for the pastor and fellow members. The former is a "drainer."

8. BE A SOUL WINNER.

One of the biggest mistakes a church member can make
is in thinking they "hired the pastor" to be the soul winner.
Every believer is a minister who is to "do the work of an
evangelist."[7]

Hell is real. It is a place of eternal regret, a place of
hopelessness, a place of separation. Every day – even at this
moment – precious souls are being swallowed into hell
through death's door. Religious and nonreligious people
alike find the same eternal destination. Why? Because religion cannot save a person, only Jesus Christ can do that.

> Jesus saith unto him, I am the way, the truth, and the
> life: no man cometh unto the Father, but by me.
>
> —John 14:6

JUST ORDINARY, SIMPLE PEOPLE

You don't have to be an official evangelist to be a soul
winner.

---

[7] 2 Timothy 4:4

Charles Finney was a lawyer.

D.L. Moody was never ordained.

Billy Sunday was a professional baseball player.

Smith Wigglesworth was a plumber.

Somebody is just waiting for you to tell them the Good News that Jesus died for their sins.

Bill Bright, founder of Campus Crusade for Christ, was not ordained.

These men, though considered great evangelists, were just ordinary, simple people like you and me. They had their personal methods of soul winning. And so do you, whether you know it or not.

Dr. Paul Walker, pastor emeritus of Mount Paran Church of God in Atlanta, Georgia, used an interesting and comfortable approach to soul winning and led thousands to Christ.[8]

Dr. Walker would meet someone, perhaps a waitress, then he'd say, "You are really a nice young lady. Where do you go to church?"

Typically, he'd get the answer, "Well, ah, ah … I don't go to church."

"Well, I'd sure love to see you at Mount Paran Church of God this Sunday, and I'll save you a spot." They would come, and Dr. Walker would win them to Christ.

---

8   Mount Paran Church of God, 2055 Mount Paran Road, Atlanta, GA 30327

You are the key to somebody coming to Christ. Simon Peter's key was his brother Andrew. Nathaniel's key was Phillip. Somebody is just waiting for you to tell them the Good News that Jesus died for their sins, and you don't have to get religious to receive forgiveness and a new start.

PROLIFIC SOUL WINNING

Do you know the most prolific method of evangelism in America today? It's called "Encouragement Evangelism," and it's simply offering to pray with a person who is facing a struggle or is in need of some kind of encouragement or support. Instead of referring to unbelievers as "non-Christians," or "sinners," Steve Sjogren, founding pastor of Vineyard Community Church in Cincinnati likes to refer to them as "pre-Christians" or "not-yet-Christians." I love that! Those are faith statements in themselves. It means they are not yet believers, but they shall be one day.

Somebody is depending on you to show them how to change their destiny.

There are three books you simply must read. I mean right now. Stop everything, run to the bookstore right now, and buy these three books:

1. *What's Your Passion* by Ken Gaub. © 2004, New Leaf Press, Green Forest, AR 72638

Ken's intriguing book shows you how to win anybody to Jesus Christ at any time, anyplace. He shows you how to win shy people, your boss, your spouse, and even people who don't want to come to the Lord. It's written in a way that is absolutely hilarious, especially when he shares the mistakes he's made in witnessing. It's an easy, enjoyable, enlightening read.

2. *Irresistible Evangelism* by Steve Sjogren, Dave Ping, and Doug Pollock. © 2004, Group Publishing. Loveland, CO 80539

This book talks about being real and non-threatening in your soul winning style.

3. *Somebody Out There Needs You* by Dave Williams. © 1991, Decapolis Publishing House, Lansing, MI 48917

My book talks about the twelve mistakes we make in evangelism. It's an easy, quick-to-read book.

If you have any trouble finding these books, call our store at 1-800-888-7284. We probably have a supply in stock.

YOU ARE A KEY TO SOMEBODY

The point is, be a soul winner. Remember, you are the key to somebody. And somebody is depending on you to show them how to change their destiny. Even if all you do is invite them to church, that's great. Keep them coming. Sooner or later, they're going to ask you questions and the Holy Spirit will give you the answers in that moment. You don't need to worry. God will back you up.

9. BRING PEOPLE TO CHURCH.

Don't be worried about what the pastor is preaching. The Holy Spirit knows how to touch people's hearts; no matter what subject he's covering.

One evening my daughter, Trina Lee, brought a friend to church to hear her dad preach. She was so excited. Then I began my sermon about "tithes and offerings." Oh, you should have seen her little face out there in the congregation that night. She was angry – really angry – at me for talking in church about money, and her disapproval was obvious every time I looked over at her. She was miserable during the entire sermon, wishing she hadn't brought her friend to church.

At the conclusion of my message, I gave a two-minute invitation for those who would like to accept Jesus Christ. Scores of people rose from their seats and walked down to pray the prayer of salvation with me. My daughter's friend came. The altar area was packed with people crying out to know Jesus. All this, and I had preached about money, stewardship, and tithing. You see, it's the anointing of the Holy Spirit, not the preacher or his preaching, that brings people to Christ.

My daughter repented and asked me to forgive her for all the dirty looks she had given me that night. She learned that you should always invite people to church no matter what the preaching subject happens to be. Besides, once people are in the building, it makes them feel comfortable about returning for another visit.

INVITE PEOPLE TO CHURCH

Invite people to church. Bring them. Offer them a ride or whatever it takes, maybe an early Sunday phone call. Just get them in the door and the Holy Spirit will do the rest.

> **And the lord said unto the servant, Go out into the highways and hedges, and compel _them_ to come in, that my house may be filled.**
>
> —Luke 14:23

10. PARTICIPATE IN SPECIAL EVENTS.

When your church is having a special event, be sure to participate in it and support it. Some folks get tired of Easter productions, but it's not about you; it's about bringing people to church. Listen. Someone's eternal destiny is hanging in the balance. It's worth watching the Easter production a second or third time for the sake of bringing someone to Jesus.

You simply cannot deny the promises in God's Word to those who are faithful with finances.

When it's time for the men's breakfast, get an extra ticket and invite someone from work.

When the women's ministry is sponsoring an event, get on board and invite all your "pre-Christian" friends and neighbors. Make every event a special soul-winning event.

11. BE FAITHFUL AND CONSISTENT IN TITHES AND OFFERINGS.

Some church members cancel out their opportunities for God's material blessings by their disobedience in tithes and offerings. But those who remember God and honor Him in tithes, offerings, alms, and first fruit gifts, have found the real secret of God's wealth-giving power. I have been sarcastically accused of being "one of those health and wealth preachers." I guess that's better than being accused of being a sickness and poverty preacher. But you simply cannot deny the promises in God's Word to those who are faithful with finances.

In fact, Jesus said:

> And if you are untrustworthy about worldly wealth, who will trust you with the true riches of heaven?
>
> —Luke 16:11 (TLB)

The tithe is the Lord's, not ours.[9] That means everyone on earth is paid 10% more than they should be, because God gives each one more than enough to obey Him with the tithe. The tithe is the first 10% of your gross income. It belongs to God.

> Will a man rob God? Yet ye have robbed me. But ye say, Wherein have we robbed thee? In tithes and offerings.
>
> Ye *are* cursed with a curse: for ye have robbed me, *even* this whole nation. Bring ye all the tithes into the storehouse, that there may be meat in mine house, and prove me now herewith, saith the LORD of hosts, if I will not open you the windows of heaven, and pour you out a blessing, that there *shall* not *be room* enough *to receive* *it*. And I will rebuke the devourer for your sakes, and he

---

9   Leciticus 27:30

> shall not destroy the fruits of your ground; neither shall your vine cast her fruit before the time in the field, saith the LORD of hosts. And all nations shall call you blessed: for ye shall be a delightsome land, saith the LORD of hosts.
>
> —Malachi 3:8-12

Offerings, our giving beyond the tithe, opens us up to receiving much back in our own lives.

> Give, and it shall be given unto you; good measure, pressed down, and shaken together, and running over, shall men give into your bosom. For with the same measure that ye mete withal it shall be measured to you again.
>
> —Luke 6:38

God actually allows you and I to chose whether we will be recipients of a big harvest or of a small harvest on the basis of our giving.

> But remember this—if you give little, you will get little. A farmer who plants just a few seeds will get only a small crop, but if he plants much, he will reap much.
>
> —2 Corinthians 9:6 (TLB)

God has even promised to give everybody some seed to sow (something to give). The person who says, "I have nothing to give God," is not telling the truth.

> God is able to make it up to you by giving you everything you need and more so that there will not only be enough for your own needs but plenty left over to give joyfully to others. It is as the Scriptures say: "The godly man gives generously to the poor. His good deeds will be an honor to him forever." For God, who gives seed to the farmer to plant, and later on good crops to harvest

and eat, will give you more and more seed to plant and will make it grow so that you can give away more and more fruit from your harvest. Yes, God will give you much so that you can give away much, and when we take your gifts to those who need them they will break out into thanksgiving and praise to God for your help.

—2 Corinthians 9:8-11 (TLB)

THE MINISTRY OF WEALTH

You may be called to the "ministry of wealth." God might want to trust you with millions of dollars. The prerequisite is to remember the Lord and put His work first with the money He's entrusted to you.

> But thou shalt remember the LORD thy God: for *it is* he that giveth thee power to get wealth, that he may establish his covenant which he sware unto thy fathers, as *it is* this day.
>
> —Deuteronomy 8:18

> Honour the LORD with thy substance, and with the firstfruits of all thine increase: So shall thy barns be filled with plenty, and thy presses shall burst out with new wine.
>
> —Proverbs 3:9-10

> But seek ye first the kingdom of God, and his right-eousness; and all these things shall be added unto you.
>
> —Matthew 6:33

But you already know this, don't you? Am I singing to the choir?

I spoke for Pastor Matthew Barnett at Angelus Temple in December of 2004. There I met a simple, but classy man named Mike Rogers. Ten years ago, Mike had only $200 remaining in his checking account. He sat in a meeting listening to Pastor Tommy Barnett, Matthew's father, sharing his vision for the International Dream Center.[10]

God spoke to Mike's heart and gently whispered, "Mike, give $200 to Pastor Tommy to help his dream come true."

"But, God," Mike protested, "$200 is all I got!"

The Lord responded, "$200 is all I asked from you."

When everyone does their part, the church doesn't have to struggle from week to week, and the church can care for the pastor and his family properly.

So, honoring the voice of the Lord to his heart, Mike wrote out a check for his last $200 and gave it to Pastor Barnett to help establish the Dream Center.

That was ten years ago. Today, Mike is writing out a monthly check for $120,000 to the Dream Center because God has blessed him so much financially. God can trust Mike with money because Mike obeys when God speaks. When we obey God first with the tithe, then offerings, we are taking the first step toward being trusted with what I call the ministry of wealth, just like Mike Rogers is enjoying today.

---

10 Los Angeles International Church and Dream Center, 2301 Bellevue Avenue, Los Angeles, CA 90026

Every pastor wishes that all the church members and attendees would tithe and give offerings. When everyone does their part, the church doesn't have to struggle from week to week, and the church can care for the pastor and his family properly.

Those who consistently tithe and bring offerings are "fuelers" for the pastor.

A *pastor's time is like gold, and the more of it he has for prayer, study, and preparation, the more you will receive.*

12

CHAPTER

PRACTICING LOVE AND WISDOM

PART 3

I was just a young pastor with colossal dreams and huge goals. I loved being in the ministry. My first year, I wanted everyone to know how accessible I was, so my office was right at the entrance of the sanctuary and had glass windows, so people could see inside. That was fine as long as our church had only 225 members, but when we started growing, the problems began.

It was a Tuesday and Mr. Cleaver (not his real name), an 83 year old former deputy sheriff, dropped by my office. What a precious man. He invited himself in and plopped down in a chair and proceeded to tell me his life story. He recounted many exciting and touching incidents while on the county police force. I heard stories about young, rowdy teenagers that he rescued from lives of alcohol and crime. Mr. Cleaver seemed to believe the best about people and took a special pride in helping struggling young people. His stories were fascinating.

After about three hours of talking, he had to get home, so he said good-bye and excused himself. On one hand, the stories were remarkable. On the other hand, I had a lot of work to catch up now, so I wouldn't make it home for dinner. But I understood.

The next day on Wednesday, while I was preparing for our Wednesday evening teaching service, I looked up, and there was Mr. Cleaver again. He walked in, sat down and began telling me all the same stories over again. It was as if he hadn't even been there the day before. I don't know if he forgot, or if he was just lonely. Yesterday, it was fascinating. I could adjust my schedule then. Today, I have a service to prepare for, and the more he talked, the heavier the weight in my shoulders became. I didn't want to be rude, but another three hours went by – that's six hours in two days of listening to what I had already heard.

Somehow God helped me to make it through the service. Mr. Cleaver wasn't there because he couldn't drive at night.

Thursday came, and I had so much to catch up on: hospital visits, phone calls, correspondence, dictations, preparation for meetings, and the list seemed endless. I heard a car pull into the parking lot, so I peaked out my window, and there he was again – Mr. Cleaver, with a big smile on his face as he headed for the office door. Without thinking, I dove under my desk and hid. He couldn't see me if he looked into the office window. I could hear muffled voices through the thin windows.

"Isn't Pastor Williams in?" asked Mr. Cleaver. "I don't see him in his office."

"Oh? I thought he was in there," responded the volunteer secretary-receptionist. "I thought sure he was in there. Maybe he slipped out for prayer and I didn't see him."

Then like a nightmare, I heard these words from Mr. Cleaver's lips: "Well, I'll just wait for him. I don't have anything else to do anyway."

Now what do I do? I asked myself. If I come out from under the desk, it'll be another three hours of hearing the same stories I've already heard two other times. I loved Mr. Cleaver and didn't want to offend him, but I had others to serve as well. And if I didn't get my work done, it could be days before my children would even see me again, I'd be getting home so late.

On the other hand, I could be curled up under here for hours while Mr. Cleaver waits for me. Oh, it was awful. And you just don't know how guilty I felt about what I was doing.

I breathed, "Thank you, Jesus," when I finally heard Mr. Cleaver leave after about thirty minutes of waiting. I surfaced from my hideout, stiff and sore, and had a heart-to-heart talk with my secretary. I instructed her to set up appointments for me on Thursday only. If it's a life or death emergency, I'll respond. Otherwise, people must make an appointment, and they will be for thirty minutes at the maximum. At thirty minutes, I instructed her to call me and let me know of my next commitment.

Some of the old timers just didn't understand that system. It upset them. Some refused and still walked in whenever they wanted. "After all, you're the pastor, and we're paying you to be available!"

I ended up putting a door on my office with no window and started to get some order to my week, even though it ruffled a lot of feathers at first.

My accountant, Scott Thompson, told me recently that if I were to spend just ten minutes with each of our 4000 + church members, doing this ten hours a week, it would take me one year and four months to meet with every member. And that is just to meet for ten minutes with our *current* constituency, not figuring times to meet with visitors and new members, let alone those who just drop in for a cup of coffee and a chat.

No wonder pastors are leaving the ministry in record numbers. They feel guilty for not being able to keep up with the impossible demands. The good news is: there is a solution for every problem and we shall get to it now.

But I felt I needed to say all this in order to preface my next two points.

12. DON'T JUST DROP BY TO SEE THE PASTOR WITHOUT AN APPOINTMENT.

It seems to me that this is a common rule of etiquette, a common courtesy. You don't just drop in to see your doctor, or your lawyer, or your accountant, or your bank president. Yet some feel they have a right as a tithe-giving member to ignore common rules of etiquette when it comes to the pastor, not even considering his schedule with others, while trying to balance it all out with his family life.

I don't know of any pastor that isn't ready to jump in on your behalf in times of emergency. But, honestly, if he's going to be successful in his work and calling, he can't be sitting around, drinking coffee and chatting with folks all day long about fishing, ball games, new cars, or ancient history. His time is like gold, and the more of it he has for prayer, study, and preparation, the more you, and all the others, will receive. Read Acts 6:1-7, and see what happened when the church leaders focused on God's priorities.

> And in those days, when the number of the disciples was multiplied, there arose a murmuring of the Grecians against the Hebrews, because their widows were neglected in the daily ministration. Then the twelve called the multitude of the disciples *unto them*, and said, It is not reason that we should leave the word of God, and serve tables. Wherefore, brethren, look ye out among you seven men of honest report, full of the Holy Ghost and wisdom, whom we may appoint over this business. But we will give ourselves continually to prayer, and to the ministry of the word. And the saying pleased the whole multitude: and they chose Stephen, a man full of faith and of the Holy Ghost, and Philip, and Prochorus, and Nicanor, and Timon, and Parmenas, and Nicolas a proselyte of Antioch: Whom they set before the apostles: and when they had prayed, they laid *their* hands on them. And the word of God increased; and the number of the disciples multiplied in Jerusalem greatly; and a great company of the priests were obedient to the faith.

> And Stephen, full of faith and power, did great wonders
> and miracles among the people.
>
> —Acts 6:1-8

Several good things happened when the church leaders prioritized prayer and God's Word (verse 4), and delegated other tasks to lay people.

1. The Word of God increased (verse 7).

2. The number of disciples multiplied (verse 7).

3. A great company of other unsaved religious leaders came to Christ (verse 7).

4. Lay people – ordinary church members, who took on some ministry responsibility for the pastor, started flowing in faith, power, wonders, and miracles (verse 8).

Why do some churches flow in God's power and others do not? I think you have the answer to that question now.

Your pastor loves you, and the greatest thing he can do for you is to spend ample time in prayer and preparation for preaching and teaching God's Word. Respect his time. Don't just drop in to chat with him for no reason. That leads us to our next point.

13. FOLLOW THE PASTOR'S ORGANIZATIONAL SYSTEM.

If a pastor is going to succeed in establishing and building healthy, growing disciples for Jesus Christ, he needs to organize a team. After all, one man simply cannot do everything and be everywhere he's wanted at the same time.

Moses learned this the hard way, thinking he was being a good shepherd to the people. He had a congregation of at least two million, and tried to meet with each person whenever they had a problem to counsel them and show them God's ways. Three negative things resulted by his management style:

First, he was about to burn out. That's right, he came to the verge of a nervous breakdown.

> *Whatever system of organization your pastor has established, follow it.*

Second, the people's needs were not being met. Moses was trying to handle it all alone. And I'm sure the people wanted to top man to deal with their situation, but, in reality, it can't be done.

Third, nobody was being trained to do what Moses did. Thus, many with gifts and talents in certain areas were remaining stunted because Moses was doing all the duties of the ministry. The attitude and mentality that insists on the pastor doing every important thing in the church will actually hinder the growth and success of the church.

Now let's look at the account from Numbers chapter eleven.

> Moses heard all the families standing around their tent doors weeping, and the anger of the Lord grew hot; Moses too was highly displeased. Moses said to the Lord, "Why pick on me, to give me the burden of a people like this? Are they *my* children? Am I their father? Is that why you have given me the job of nursing them

along like babies until we get to the land you promised their ancestors? Where am I supposed to get meat for all these people? For they weep to me saying, 'Give us meat!'

I can't carry this nation by myself! The load is far too heavy! If you are going to treat me like this, please kill me right now; it will be a kindness! Let me out of this impossible situation!" Then the Lord said to Moses, "Summon before me seventy of the leaders of Israel; bring them to the Tabernacle, to stand there with you. I will come down and talk with you there, and I will take of the Spirit which is on you and will put it upon them also; they shall bear the burden of the people along with you, so that you will not have the task alone.

—Numbers 11:10-17 (TLB)

And Exodus chapter eighteen:

The next day Moses sat as usual to hear the people's complaints against each other, from morning to evening. When Moses' father-in-law saw how much time this was taking, he said, "Why are you trying to do all this alone, with people standing here all day long to get your help?" "Well, because the people come to me with their disputes, to ask for God's decisions," Moses told him. "I am their judge, deciding who is right and who is wrong, and instructing them in God's ways. I apply the laws of God to their particular disputes." "It's not right!" his father-in-law exclaimed. "You're going to wear yourself out—and if you do, what will happen to the people? Moses, this job is too heavy a burden for you to try to handle all by yourself.

Now listen, and let me give you a word of advice, and God will bless you: Be these people's lawyer—their representative before God—bringing him their questions to decide; you will tell them his decisions, teaching them God's laws, and showing them the principles of godly living.

"Find some capable, godly, honest men who hate bribes, and appoint them as judges, one judge for each 1000 people; he in turn will have ten judges under him, each in charge of a hundred; and under each of them will be two judges, each responsible for the affairs of fifty people; and each of these will have five judges beneath him, each counseling ten persons.

Let these men be responsible to serve the people with justice at all times. Anything that is too important or complicated can be brought to you. But the smaller matters they can take care of themselves. That way it will be easier for you because you will share the burden with them. If you follow this advice, and if the Lord agrees, you will be able to endure the pressures, and there will be peace and harmony in the camp."

—Exodus18:13-23 (TLB)

This is called organizing for success, peace, and harmony in the church. Every pastor needs to appoint assistants to help him in the work of ministry. Some assistant ministers are paid and some are anointed lay leaders.

Whatever system of organization your pastor has established, follow it.

If you need an appointment, don't demand to see the pastor first. Follow the established order. Go first to a fellowship group leader, or Sunday school teacher. If you don't get the help you need, ask the leader to take you to the next level, perhaps a department director. If that doesn't work, next have the department director take you to an assistant minister, then an associate minister, then finally the pastor.

If the pastor makes himself available to anybody at anytime for any reason, the church will suffer and stagnate. His focus should be on prayer, study, and training God's people to do the work of the ministry.

> He is the one who gave these gifts to the church: the apostles, the prophets, the evangelists, and the pastors and teachers. Their responsibility is to equip God's people to do his work and build up the church, the body of Christ, until we come to such unity in our faith and knowledge of God's Son that we will be mature and full grown in the Lord, measuring up to the full stature of Christ.
>
> —Ephesians 4:11-13 (NLT)

Follow the pastor's system.

14. DON'T SEND THE PASTOR LONG, HAND-WRITTEN NOTES.

These are hard to read and burdensome. When you write, do so succinctly and neatly. It will help your pastor and he'll appreciate your thoughtfulness. Don't be afraid to write him. Your note or letter will bless his day. Just make sure it's neat and brief.

15. BE A TROUBLE-UNTANGLER; NOT A TROUBLEMAKER.

You will be remembered in this life for one of two things: the problems you have solved, or the problems you have created. I call problem solvers "trouble untanglers" because that describes what Jesus does for people with the sin problem.

> He that committeth sin is of the devil; for the devil sinneth from the beginning. For this purpose the Son of God was manifested, that he might destroy the works of the devil.
>
> —1 John 3:8

Think of it. The Son of God was manifested, that he might destroy the works of the devil. The word: "destroy" means to "untangle" or "undo." Sin has brought plenty of tangles and entanglements to people's lives. And our wonderful Savior came to untangle the tangled-up mess sin and the devil have caused in a person's life. Jesus is the Great Trouble Untangler.

It's not wrong to bring a problem to the pastor — something that needs attention. But if you want to be a "fueler" and not a "drainer" for you pastor, then come with some possible solutions for the problem. I used to hear so often things like this: "Pastor, we have a problem over here, and I really don't know what the solution is." True leaders will always bring solutions. They are trouble-untanglers. Be a trouble-untangler.

And here's what Paul said about troublemakers:

> A man that is an heretick after the first and second admonition reject; Knowing that he that is such is subverted, and sinneth, being condemned of himself.
>
> —Titus 3:10-11

A "heretick" is a divisive troublemaker. A troublemaker is to be warned once, then again, and if he doesn't stop causing trouble in the church, he is to be asked to leave. It's exciting and adventurous to find ways of untangling troubles.

16. ALWAYS SPEAK WELL OF YOUR PASTOR AND YOUR CHURCH.

Solomon said the power of life and death is in the tongue.[11] It's true. I've seen the power of the tongue being used for good or for evil over and over again in the past three

---

[11] Proverbs 18:21

decades of ministry. Jesus said, "Judge not, that you be not judged." The word "judge" in this instance means, "condemn."

Our wonderful Savior came to untangle the tangled-up mess sin and the devil have caused in a person's life.

There are those who use their tongues to condemn others, criticize, point out faults, discourage, belittle, and put down. On the other hand, there are those who seem to always use their tongues to bless, encourage, inspire, and speak well of others. It's all a matter of choice.

I've seen firsthand how a church can blossom and grow when the members are speaking well of their pastor and their church. People that speak good things are usually the same people that lead many to Christ and to the church.

I've also seen how speaking negatively about the pastor and the church can hurt the families of those who are engaged in it. For example, Mr. and Mrs. Osbourne (not their real names) always pointed out their pastor's faults at the dinner table in the presence of their two children. They forced their daughter to be in the church Missionette program (like girl scouts) and their son to be in Royal Rangers (like boy scouts). Yet they couldn't quit pointing out all the weaknesses in the pastor's preaching, his wrong use of certain words, and anything that bothered them about the church.

I remember both of these children when they were active in the youth ministry. They never seemed to have much respect for authority. When they became older teenagers, they both left the church, thumbing their nose at the leadership. It's no wonder. It could be predicted. All they heard growing up was how "Mickey Mouse" that sermon was, or how "rinky-dink" that service was. They had no respect for any leadership in the church, and it transferred to social life as well. No respect for teachers, police, elected officials, or others in authority.

Without going into the painful details, let me simply say that both of the children's lives fell apart as they became entangled in the worst sins you can imagine. When they needed help and guidance, there was nobody they could turn to because they had heard mom and dad's brutally negative words all their young lives about every pastor they had ever known. They had no respect or confidence in anyone who represented God in any way.

If you want to be a "fueler" and not a "drainer" for your pastor, then come with possible solutions to a problem.

The pain those parents live with today is almost unbearable. They lost both of their children to wickedness, and don't know how it could have happened to them, such a prominent church-going family. Even to this day, they haven't figured it out, and continue to criticize and condemn men and women of God.

But when you look for good things to say about your church and your pastor, you'll begin to actually see your own excitement building. You'll be enthused and motivated to bring many friends and family members to Christ and to your church. And God will show you how to reach them. It's like a miracle. Speak well of your church and your pastor.

17. WALK IN LOVE AND WISDOM TOWARD ALL PEOPLE.

We are talking about practical things that will help your pastor succeed. Here's a big one: walk in love and wisdom toward all people inside the church and outside the church.

You may not realize it, but you are a "marketer" for your church. Others will get their view and opinions about your pastor and your church based upon your attitude and actions.

Joe Girard is the world's greatest salesman, a title never beaten as attested by the Guinness Book of World Records. In his book, *How to Sell Anything to Anybody*[12], Joe talks about "250 rule." The 250 rule states any one person will affect 250 others. That means that 250 people will get their opinion of your pastor and your church from you. If you are full of love, walking in wisdom toward all, the word will get out to 250 others. If you act like a snob, never help anyone, treat people rudely, 250 others will get an

> *Walk in love and wisdom toward all people inside the church and outside the church.*

---

12 Girard, Joe, *How To Sell Anything To Anybody* 1986, Warner Books, New York, NY 10020

image of your pastor and church based on your attitudes and behavior.

Walk in Christ's joy, and let it show. Put yourself in other people's shoes. Be polite, courteous, kind, and gentle, even to those who are different than you or difficult to deal with. For every one person you bless, 250 others will hear about it. For every one positive testimony about your church you share, 250 others, most of whom you don't even know, will find out about it.

> *People that speak good things are usually the same people that lead many to Christ and to the church.*

While attending a conference where Dr. R.T. Kendall, pastor for 25 years of Westminster Chapel in London, England was speaking, I wrote down something he said. He told us about a book that every pastor should read. He warned that it's not a Christian book, but the principles are biblically sound. The book is *How to Win Friends and Influence People* by Dale Carnegie.[13]

If you want to know how to walk in love and wisdom toward all people, get a copy of Carnegie's book, read it, and apply the principles.

18. Don't be a distraction.

If your church allows infants in the adult service, sit in the back seats and go into the foyer if the baby creates a fuss.

---

13 Carnegie, Dale, How to Win Friends and Influence People 1936, Simon and Schuster, Inc. New York, NY 10020

If everyone is worshipping in a silent manner, don't be the loud, overbearing voice of praise, or you'll become a distraction to others.

Don't make weird gyrations in church during singing, praise, and worship times. This draws attention to you and distracts from the One who is to have preeminence – Jesus Christ!

Years ago I loved to attend a small church about 12 miles north of my home. The pastor regularly would call us to the altar for times of prayer at the close of the service. It was a precious time of prayer and reflection. That is, until Deacon Chester showed up. He'd be screeching praises to the Lord in maximum volume, then, he'd start methodically clapping his hands while people were trying to tenderly seek the Lord. It was so annoying and distracting that I wanted to scream and run. He was innocently unaware that he was breaking the holy atmosphere with his distracting practices every time.

19. DON'T GIVE THE YOUR PASTOR YOUR PERSONAL OPINIONS, LIKES AND DISLIKES, MASKED AS A PROPHETIC WORD FROM THE LORD.

Pastors receive letters, some daily or weekly, that contain complaints in the form of a spiritual prophecy or "word from heaven."

"God told me to tell you ..."

"God showed me ..."

"Pastor, I received a word from the Lord about so and so, and He showed me such and such ..."

"Pastor, the Lord told me to warn you ..."

"The Lord showed me clearly that He is displeased with the music and if you don't go back to singing hymns, He is going to ..."

Others will get their view and opinions about your pastor and your church based upon your attitude.

Some of these people sound like Job's friends. This is a childish way of trying to exert control over the man of God in forcing one's own opinions.

Now, if you have relationship with the pastor as a solid prayer partner, of course you may speak to him what the Lord is laying on your heart. But if you are not one of the pastor's intercessors, and he doesn't know you well, don't presume to speak for the Lord into his life.

If you'd like to do an in-depth study on how God feels about these kinds of things, please get a copy of my book, *The Jezebel Spirit.*[14]

---

[14] Williams, Dave, The Jezebel Spirit, 2003, Decapolis Publishing House, Lansing, MI 48917

Your pastor loves you and watches over your soul. Don't take yourself and your family out from under that protection.

13

PRACTICING LOVE AND WISDOM

PART 4

One morning I was reading my devotions from Eugene H. Peterson's, *The Message Bible* [15] and stumbled upon a verse that I highlighted and marked as "The Pastor's Cry." Here it is from Psalm 56:1-3:

> Take my side, God – I'm getting kicked around, stomped on every day. Not a day goes by but somebody beats me up; They make it their duty to beat me up. When I get really afraid I come to you in trust.

It's a mystery to me why some people seem to make it their career to bring discouragement and trouble to the pastor. I know it's not the majority, but there are times it seems that way to the pastor.

---

[15] Peterson, Eugene H., *The Message* Remix: The Bible in Contemporary Language,

Years ago a young man I didn't recognize showed up at our Thursday evening prayer meeting. Before the meeting, he walked up to me and contorted some strange gyrations, and in a deep, falsetto-like voice pronounced, "Thus saith the Lord, I have called thee to be my captain over this city, and thou shalt lead an army of 50,000, saith the Lord."

> *Oh, how a pastor needs members who will make visitors feel welcome regardless of how they look or act.*

I felt no particular witness; nonetheless, I thanked him for his kind words.

Later, while everyone was worshipping, he piped up again with a booming, authoritative voice and bellowed, "Thus saith the Lord, you all think you are in the Spirit but I say unto you that you are all in the flesh ..." At that point I stopped him from interrupting our time of prayer and worship.

After the prayer meeting, he marched up to me and demanded to know, "Why did you stop my prophecy?"

"Because it wasn't from God, but from your imagination," I told him.

He started the contortions and weird expressions again, and droned, "Thus saith the Lord, because you have not received my anointed prophet, your church shall now dwindle down to only twelve, and thy children shall be dressed in rags, saith the Lord of hosts."

Imagine that, I thought. Less than an hour ago he said I'd lead an army of 50,000. Now he declared it would dwindle to twelve.

Needless to say, I invited him to leave and not return. He did leave but not until he had tried to influence dozens of people against me.

I understand the struggles pastor's face, of which most people have no idea. And I know what it's like to have "drainers," and what it's like to have "fuelers."

Drainers drain. Fuelers fuel.

This book is about fueling the pastor for success. Now, let's look at some more practical expressions of love and wisdom you can apply for your pastor's success.

20. BE GENTLE WITH CHURCH VISITORS.

People who visit the church already feel awkward and apprehensive. We don't want to add to that with our stares, glares, and unwise words.

Jill, a precious young lady was invited to church several times by her neighborhood friend. Jill had never been to church in her life except for weddings and funerals. Finally she came one Sunday wearing a cowgirl shirt, blue jean pants, and heavy make up. When she went into the lady's room she overheard some women talking. "Did you see that harlot-looking woman wearing blue jeans in church today?" "Oh yes, I wonder what *her kind* is doing in our church."

That was twenty-two years ago, and Jill never returned to church.

That's one story. Here's another. Mary came to church for years without her husband. He had no desire to attend church or to be a Christian. One time when he faced a crisis in his life, he did come to church with his wife. When one of the men in the church spotted him, he went and sat right behind them. He leaned forward and in a condescending manner, told the husband, "It's about time you came to church with your wife. What kind of man are you anyway, letting her come to church by herself all these years? You should be ashamed of yourself. When the pastor gives the invitation at the close of his sermon, you better get up to that altar and be a real man. If you don't you may end up in a casket and you'll be blistering in hell."

Those who sit in the front rows seem to get more from the messages and times of worship.

The man walked out of the church and never returned again.

These are two true stories from my experience as a pastor.

Oh, how a pastor needs members who will make visitors feel welcome regardless of how they look or act. Try to remember your first few times in church. How did you feel? For me, I'm thankful people in the church accepted me, loved me, encouraged me, and didn't make me feel like an outsider. I didn't always look right or act right, but God was changing me day by day, from glory to glory. Be kind to people and withhold your judgment and critical remarks. Let God do His precious work in their lives without your interference.

21. SIT IN THE FRONT PEWS.

Why is it that most everywhere in churches the front pews are empty every Sunday? This may sound strange, but those in the front rows seem to get more from the messages and times of worship. I don't know why that is, unless the anointing is richer and undiluted up close.

God requires a visible identification with a local expression of Christ's body (the local church).

22. BECOME AN OFFICIAL MEMBER OF YOUR CHURCH.

There are always those who believe they are "God's gift to the entire body of Christ," so they hop from church to church. Sometimes they get their spiritual feeding from Christian television, and sense no need to be an active part of a local expression of Christ's body. They wear those "spiritual diapers" while they try to project a deep, spiritual aura of holiness.

Only members are part of the life of a body. Your church is a microcosm of the body of Christ. Mere attendees are never a part of the life of a church because the Bible teaches that life is in the blood (Leviticus 17:14). Attendees are important. They are like the jewelry that adorns the body, but they are not really part of the body until they determine to make an official commitment to the church through membership. Read I Corinthians 12, Romans 12, and Ephesians 4. These passages speak of the body of Christ, and show the importance of being a member.

Every born again person is a member of the invisible, universal body of Christ. But God requires a visible identification with a local expression of Christ's body (the local church). For example, He commanded water baptism to provide a *visible expression* of a believer dying to himself and rising in the power of Christ. And a commitment to the visible expression of Christ's body – the local church – shows a genuine identification with the invisible, universal body of Christ (His Church).

23. REALIZE THE PASTOR IS HUMAN AND HAS SOME FRAILTIES AND FAULTS LIKE ANYONE ELSE.

Your pastor has dreams, desires, and emotions too. Sometimes he makes mistakes or says stupid things. Go easy on him. If you spoke publicly as much as he does, you'd probably make a few mistakes here and there too.

> Blessed *are* the merciful: for they shall obtain mercy.
>
> —Matthew 5:7

> Don't criticize, and then you won't be criticized. For others will treat you as you treat them. And why worry about a speck in the eye of a brother when you have a board in your own? Should you say, 'Friend, let me help you get that speck out of your eye,' when you can't even see because of the board in your own? Hypocrite! First get rid of the board. Then you can see to help your brother.
>
> —Matthew 7:1-5 (TLB)

24. DON'T GIVE HIM A BOOK OR AUDIO MESSAGE TO REVIEW AND THEN ASK HIM TO GET BACK TO YOU WITH HIS OPINION.

Pastors get things every week people want him to read or listen to and evaluate. Sometimes the pastor will have time, sometimes he won't. I know for me, I have at least (and this is no exaggeration) a thousand books and tapes people have wanted me to examine over the past twenty-some years. When I get another one, I put it on the bottom of the pile and when I can get to it I will. It may take me another fifty years. I've learned that I simply cannot do everything people would like me to do. And neither can your pastor.

Imagine if a hundred people brought their pastor a book and demanded an opinion by Sunday!

If you buy him a book, make sure he knows it's a gift for him. Don't ask him to return it and don't ask him to give you a book report after reading it. That's unfair and selfish. It might be nice for him to read at his leisure and enjoy it, without the pressure of having to report back.

Can you imagine if a hundred people brought their pastor a book and demanded an opinion by next Sunday? Everybody thinks they are the only one laying a chore on the pastor, but in reality, there are usually many more than one. And it all piles up.

I finally took all the books and tapes that were piling up in my study, filed them in boxes and had them placed in a storage room until I can get to them in the order in which they came.

Pastors are busier than ever today. Try not to lay more burdens on them if you want them to succeed in their ministries.

25. INTRODUCE HIM PROPERLY.

Even if you are on a first name basis with your pastor, it reflects style, class, and proper etiquette to introduce him by his proper title.

I was conducting a wedding rehearsal one time when almost the entire wedding party was made up of people who had never met me. Everyone seemed shocked when the wedding consultant announced, "Dave, come on up here and pray before we get started." The bride and groom were embarrassed that someone would be so ill mannered to call their pastor by his first name in front of their families.

> *It is proper etiquette and shows real style when you introduce your pastor properly.*

It's proper etiquette, and shows real style when you introduce your pastor properly.

For example, "Mother, I'd like you to meet my pastor, Doctor James McDermott." Or, "I'd like to introduce you to our pastor, Reverend Don Wolcutt." Or, "Dad, this is Reverend Edward Smith, the minister of music at Calvary Church."

If the pastor feels comfortable, it is up to him to respond by saying something like, "Most people call me Pastor John or just John is fine."

26. DON'T EXPECT YOUR PASTOR TO BE IN ATTENDANCE FOR EVERY MINISTRY OR MEETING.

Pastors who try to be like the Holy Spirit, quickly burn out. It's physically impossible for him to be in more than one place at a time.

I conducted a congregational survey one October to help me fine-tune some ministries around the church. The survey went to about 3000 people and came back with plenty of helpful comments. But some of the comments were:

"Pastor, I think you need to attend the men's meetings"

"The pastor should attend all the Monday night Alpha banquets."

"It would be nice if the pastor would come to the 50+ meetings regularly."

"Pastor, will you please come to our fellowship meetings in our home?"

Listen, dear one. If the pastor has to attend everything, then he doesn't need any staff members or lay leaders in the church. And if the pastor is expected to attend every ministry, he'll have to cut many of the ministries just so he can make time to be there. If you wish your church to stay small and if you wish to be a "drainer" instead of a "fueler," then simply demand that the pastor be in attendance for everything that's important to you.

Maturity is when you realize your limitations without feeling guilty. It is also maturity when you understand that your pastor is simply one person doing his best to make disciples and multiply the church ministries in the community, and cannot possibly attend everything.

27. NEVER RECEIVE AN ACCUSATION AGAINST YOUR PASTOR THAT IS NOT SUBSTANTIATED AND BACKED UP BY TWO OR THREE CREDIBLE WITNESSES.

> Against an elder receive not an accusation, but before two or three witnesses.
>
> —1 Timothy 5:19

It is maturity when you understand that your pastor is simply one person and can't attend everything.

Every church has its disgruntled former members or employees. They need to justify their own feelings of failure, so they typically blame or accuse the pastor. Others are just plain wicked and forever dreaming up some charge against a man of God. They seem to ignore the solemn warning of the Scriptures:

> Touch not mine anointed, and do my prophets no harm.
>
> —Psalms 105:15

Here's what David said about people like this:

> You are sharp as a tack in plotting your evil tricks. How you love wickedness—far more than good! And lying

more than truth! You love to slander—you love to say
anything that will do harm, O man with the lying tongue.
But God will strike you down, pull you from your home,
and drag you away from the land of the living.

—Psalms 52:2-5 (TLB)

Oftentimes when members refuse discipline and leave
the church in bitterness, they will create slanderous stories,
thinking they are protecting their own reputation. It happens almost one hundred per cent of the time. They don't
want others to think *they* are the problem, so they rewrite
history, placing the blame or accusation on the pastor, elder,
or someone in the church with whom they disagreed. Don't
fall for this trap.

28. BE DISCERNING.

Be like a tree planted by
the waters, not like a reed
blowing in the wind. Weird
doctrines are always blowing
through town, designed to
"make merchandise of you."

Be like a tree planted by the waters, not a reed blowing in the wind.

Not too long ago an old
heresy resurfaced in the
body of Christ. I've seen this particular one three times in
my own life appear in different packaging, with new teachers, and the claim of a fresh revelation.

I started getting requests from certain members for a
transfer of their membership. They thanked me for leading
them as far as I could, but now, in order for them to grow in
the Lord, they needed to be under an apostle instead of just

a pastor. All of their letters sounded exactly alike. They were on different paper, had different penmanship and different phrases, but all had the same message. "I can't grow unless I have an apostle."

After a little research and investigation, I discovered that a former member of our church began studying under a man who was a self-proclaimed apostle. He was influencing our members to join his new church under apostolic leadership.

The self-proclaimed apostle had previously been part of a denominational group; he fell into moral problems, refused discipline from his elders, and disappeared from the scene. Two years later he emerged with a freshly written book, promoting himself as an apostle and expert of the new order. Throughout the book he put emotional hooks to snag undiscerning Christians into joining his "movement." After reading the book, people became dissatisfied with their pastors and their churches because there were no visible apostles.

Your pastor's family faces pressures that ordinary families do not.

I discovered that this new "movement" was set up like a multi-level marketing system. Each apostle in the hierarchy received a portion of the member's tithes and offerings. The more groups you could sign up under you, the more profit there was for the apostle. The whole thing was bizarre. No wonder they were actively and aggressively targeting church members – more money for themselves! I've seen this particular doctrine come and go twice before in the past decades, only each time it came with a different title and different packaging.

Be discerning. Pray things through to victory before you act on some emotionally appealing, but scripturally unsound doctrine.

> But there were false prophets also among the people, even as there shall be false teachers among you, who privily shall bring in damnable heresies, even denying the Lord that bought them, and bring upon themselves swift destruction. And many shall follow their pernicious ways; by reason of whom the way of truth shall be evil spoken of. And through covetousness shall they with feigned words make merchandise of you: whose judgment now of a long time lingereth not, and their damnation slumbereth not.
>
> —2 Peter 2:1-3

Jesus paid a high price for your liberty and freedom. Don't allow someone with whom you have no real relationship to rob it from you. Your pastor loves you and watches over your soul. Don't take yourself and your family out from under that protection.

29. BE THOUGHTFUL AND CONSIDERATE OF YOUR PASTOR AND HIS FAMILY.

The pastor's family faces pressures that ordinary families do not. Not only does he live in a proverbial glass house, but his family lives there with him. Let me give you some ways to be thoughtful and considerate:

Cheer him on. Send him a short, encouraging note once in awhile.

Don't use his children to send messages to the pastor. They are children, not couriers. Don't say to them, "Tell your dad…" This puts unfair pressure on them, and makes them feel like running.

Encourage his wife. She shares the load right along with her husband. She has sacrificed more than you know to be in the ministry. Not that she complains about it, she probably does not. She probably counts it a great privilege to serve with her husband in Christ's calling. Offer her encouraging words. Don't expect her to oversee the women's ministry, music ministry, or other areas that perhaps previous pastor's wives oversaw. Give her a nice, non-personal gift once in awhile; perhaps a gift certificate or money to buy a new outfit.

> *Encourage your pastor's wife. She shares the load right along with her husband. She has sacrificed more than you know.*

If you give a gift to the pastor for Christmas or a birthday, make sure it's not something personal, like a tie. He may not like the style you selected, but feel obligated to wear it. A gift certificate is a great gift. That way he can pick out something for himself, and will be just perfect. He'll thank you for it.

30. STAY TEACHABLE AND PLIABLE.

"When you're green, you grow. When you're ripe, you rot." Don't be a ripe know-it-all.

Take notes when your pastor is preaching or teaching. It looks sharp. And it provides a good example to new believers and also projects the image of being teachable and humble.

If you disagree with the pastor on something, take time to make it a matter of prayer. Listen to the Holy Spirit. Be pliable. If the pastor is wrong, he'll take correction as long as he knows you have his best interest at heart.

> *Take notes while your pastor is preaching or teaching. It provides a good example for new believers.*

SUMMING IT UP

There. I've given you thirty rapid-fire ways to be a blessing – a "fueler" – to your pastor. The list is not exhaustive, but a good start.

Pastors are people. Most of them want to accomplish something great with God in their particular communities. With your help, your pastor can reflect the light of God your church has prayed for. Pastors, like others, grow in an atmosphere of love, acceptance, and grace.

Will you be a "fueler" for your pastor? Will you help him succeed in his special calling from God? I believe you will.

T here are few people as
important as your pastor,
and he needs your help to win
your community to Christ.

THE LAST WORD

It has been wonderful to share with you principles for helping your pastor succeed. If you have felt frustrated about your role in the local church, I trust that this book has given you keys to unlock the doors to effective ministry.

We have discussed:

- Moving from the multitude to the inner circle
- Echoing the pastor's vision
- Watching out for wolves
- Keeping unity
- Finding your unique place
- Developing a successful Christian home
- Enforcing Christ's victory
- Engaging in corporate spiritual warfare
- Being an effective number two
- Practicing the principles of love and wisdom

In its own way each of these subjects will help you to hold up your pastor's arms, promote his vision, and strengthen the church. You will find that your own ministry will grow as well.

There are few people as important as your pastor, and he needs your help to win your community to Christ. The sooner you learn these lessons, the more people you will win, and the more effective your church will be at producing mature, soul-winning believers.

These straightforward principles will help you and your pastor attain the highest goals God has in His heart for you, and you will become a spiritual powerhouse in your community.

Parents
~~News~~

WFRN.com
7,9   2,5,7

APPENDIX I

PRAYER PLAN FOR MY PASTOR
BEFORE HE MINISTERS

PRE-MINISTRY

- Pray that the Holy Spirit and angels will go ahead of my pastor to prepare the way:

- In his study and preparation time

- In people's hearts to whom he will be ministering

- Pray as the Lord leads you in this area for the choir, band, worship leaders, greeters, ushers, care givers, youth and children's ministries, and other ministers and ministries in the church.

MINISTRY TIME

- Pray that the glory and presence of the Lord will fill the service (Psalm 72:19).

- Pray that the Name, Power, and Authority of Jesus Christ will be exalted.

- Pray that Pastor's time of ministry will be the most anointed and memorable ever in the hearts and lives of those who will be attending.

- Pray that each attendee will have an authentic renewal in the Spirit.

- Pray that Pastor's ministry time will be so refreshing, it will be spiritually like:

  -Rivers of great joy

  -Pools of heaven's blessings

  -Seas of mercy and grace from God

  -Oceans of anointing

  -Lakes of great refreshing waters

WARFARE

- Bind and subdue:

  -Critical spirits

  -Distracting spirits

  -Judgmental spirits

  -Religious spirits

  -Argumentative spirits

  -Rebellious spirits

  -Hostile spirits

  -Jezebel spirits

  -Jealous spirits

- Pray the protection of angels over Pastor

- Pray as the Lord leads you in the act of spiritual warfare

- Release from Heaven:

  -Holy Spirit Anointing

  -Blessings to all who attend

  -Deliverance, Healing, Anointing, Revelation, Divine
  Rest, Salvation

- Plead the Blood of Jesus over the service, the attendees,
  my pastor, and anyone who may be in the service "by
  accident."

- Pray the "Prayer of Jabez" over Pastor, the attendees, and
  the entire service.

- Pray that Pastor's message and ministry time will be
  packed with revelation, insight, and supernatural gifts of
  the Holy Spirit.

- Pray that each person's eyes and ears will be opened to
  see and hear wondrous things from God's Word and
  God's Spirit during Pastor's ministry time.

FOR PASTOR

- Cause Pastor to hear from Heaven alone.

- Cause Pastor to be so full of the Holy Spirit and His
  Words that they'll be like a stream of vibrant, healing,
  energizing waters in the desert of people's lives.

- Cause Pastor to speak in a compelling, magnetic, warm,
  and charismatic manner that will build bridges to these
  precious people.

- Grant Pastor extraordinary favor with both those who are saved and those who are not yet part of God's Kingdom.

- Multiply Your anointing, oh Lord, upon my pastor as he ministers.

- Help my pastor to radiate warmth, love, and joy with the compassion of Jesus, Himself.

- Grant my pastor words of knowledge, words of wisdom, prophetic words, along with a genuine teaching anointing.

- Help my pastor to be bold, confident, and full of faith, exuding with love, peace and joy.

- Cause my pastor to be received as an angel (like St. Paul described).

- Pray as the Holy Spirit leads you in this area.

RESULTS EXPECTED

- The results and fruit of this meeting to reverberate into the future.

- That every attendee will be encouraged, motivated, and inspired to fulfill their call and reach their greatest potential in Christ.

- That ministries and personal lives will grow and prosper as a result of this meeting.

- Marriages and godly alliances will be renewed and strengthened.

- That a fresh release of love will be dispatched onto the body of Christ.

- People will be lifted to a new height in their walk with Jesus; the lost will be saved, the bound will go free, the sick will be healed, the poor will receive the Good News.

- Pray that prayers will be answered speedily in the lives of the attendees.

- That great reward will come to those who pray fervently for this meeting.

- Above all, that honor and glory will be brought to our Lord, Jesus Christ!

APPENDIX II

The Prayer of Jabez for My Pastor

Lord, Bless My Pastor Greatly ...
In his home
In his ministry
In his personal life
In his times of study and preparation
In his speaking and preaching assignments and in his travels

Put Your Hand Upon My Pastor ...
Anoint him powerfully
To do more than he can do alone
To achieve more than he can achieve
To see results in his ministry that are supernatural
To touch people's lives in a unique way
To minister in an unforgettable way

Enlarge My Pastor's Territory ...
Personally and in his ministry
In his influence among common people
In his influence among ministers

In the distribution of his books and recorded messages
In his effect upon millions of lives
In his preaching and teaching ministry
In our church
In our community
Prosper My Pastor in every way

Keep My Pastor from All Evil ...
People with ill motives
Wicked people with evil designs
Gossiping tongues and rumor-mongers
Hold him close and protect him from any plan of the devil
In thoughts, words, and deeds

Help My Pastor to Never Cause Hurt ...
To himself
To his family
To his church
To fellow believers
To fellow ministers
To the body of Christ in general

*Thank you, Lord, for hearing this prayer
for my pastor, and for answering it
and blessing me for interceding.*

RECOMMENDED READING

Under Cover by John BeVere, 2001, Nelson Books, Nashville, TN 37214

Twelve Ways to be a Blessing to Your Church by Kate McVeigh, 2003, Harrison House, Inc., Tulsa, OK 74137

How to Keep the Pastor You Love by Jane Rubietta, 2002, InterVarsity Press, Downers Grove, IL 60515

Pastors at Greater Risk by H.B. London and Neil B. Wiseman, 2003, Regal Books, Ventura, CA 93003

Your Pastor: Preyed On or Prayed For? by Terry Teykl, 1997, Prayer Point Press, Muncie, IN 47304

Possessing the Gates of the Enemy by Cindy Jacobs, 1991, 1994, Chosen Books, Grand Rapids, MI 49516

Partners in Prayer by John Maxwell, 1996, Thomas Nelson Publishers, Nashville, TN 37214

The Jezebel Spirit by Dave Williams, 2003, Decapolis Publishing Group, Lansing, MI 48917

What's Your Passion? by Ken Gaub, 2004, New Leaf Press, Green Forest, AR 72638

Irresistible Evangelism by Steve Sjogren, Dave Ping, and Doug Pollock, 2004, Group Publishing, Loveland, CO 80539

ABOUT
THE AUTHOR
AND RELATED
MINISTRIES

ABOUT THE AUTHOR

Dr. Dave Williams is pastor of Mount Hope Church and International Outreach Ministries, with world headquarters in Lansing, Michigan. He has served for over 20 years, leading the church in Lansing from 226 to over 4000 today. Dave sends trained ministers into unreached cities to establish disciple-making churches, and, as a result, today has "branch" churches in the United States, Philippines, and in Africa.

Dave is the founder and president of Mount Hope Bible Training Institute, a fully accredited institute for training ministers and lay people for the work of the ministry. He has authored over 55 books including the fifteen-time best seller, *The New Life...The Start of Something Wonderful* (with over 2,000,000 books sold), and more recently, *The Miracle Results of Fasting, The Road To Radical Riches,* and *Angels-They Are Watching You!*

The Pacesetter's Path telecast is Dave's weekly television program seen over a syndicated network of secular stations, and nationally over the *Sky Angel* satellite system. He is also seen worldwide on the *TCT* Satellite System, receiving over 1,000 salvation calls to the prayer center weekly. Dave has produced over 125 audio cassette programs including the nationally acclaimed *School of Pacesetting Leadership* which is being used as a training program in churches around the United States, and in Bible Schools in South Africa, South America, Mexico, and the Philippines. He is a popular speaker at conferences, seminars, and conventions. His speaking ministry has taken him across America, Africa, Europe, Asia, and other parts of the world.

Along with his wife, Mary Jo, Dave established The Dave and Mary Jo Williams Charitable Mission (Strategic Global Mission), a mission's ministry for providing scholarships to pioneer pastors and grants to inner-city children's ministries.

He travels with his family and enjoys vacationing in Florida. Dave and Mary Jo own *Sun Prime Equities*, a Florida island condo enterprise.

Dave received his doctorate of ministry from Pacific International University in 2004.

Dave's articles and reviews have appeared in national magazines such as *Advance, The Pentecostal Evangel, Ministries Today, The Lansing Magazine, The Detroit Free Press* and others.

During his time of study, he developed curriculum for *The School of Intercessors* and *The School of Successful Church Planting*. Both are being taught in churches across the United States. Dave, as a private pilot, flies for fun. He is married, has two grown children, and lives in Delta Township, Michigan.

You may write to Pastor Dave Williams:

P.O. Box 80825
Lansing, MI 48908-0825

Please include your special prayer requests when you write, or you may call the Mount Hope Global Prayer Center: (517) 327-PRAY

For a catalog of products, call:

1-517-321-2780 or

1-800-888-7284

or visit us on the web at:

www.mounthopechurch.org

Gilead Healing Center

HEALING CENTER

- The Place Of Another Chance
- Training For The Healing Ministry

- *Prayer*
- *Nutrition*
- *Counseling*
- *Medical*

517-321-2780

We're here for you!
Lansing, Michigan

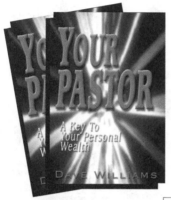

When you face a struggle...
When you need a miracle...

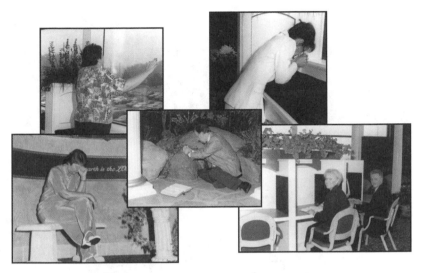

...we'll stand with you in prayer.

GLOBAL PRAYER CENTER

We believe Jesus Christ is the same yesterday, today and forever (Hebrews 13:6).

Our prayer partners will agree with you in prayer for your miracle (Matthew 18:18-19).

Call Anytime
(517) 327-PRAY

The Mount Hope Global Prayer Center in Lansing, Michigan

OTHER OFFERINGS FROM DECAPOLIS PUBLISHING

FOR YOUR SPIRITUAL GROWTH

Here's the help you need for your spiritual journey. These books will encourage you, and give you guidance as you seek to draw close to Jesus and learn of Him. Prepare yourself for fantastic growth!

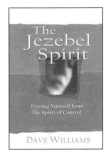

RADICAL FASTING
How would you like to achieve your dreams at "break-neck" speed? Radical fasting may be your key!

REGAINING YOUR SPIRITUAL MOMENTUM
Use this remarkable book as your personal street map to regain your spiritual momentum.

THE JEZEBEL SPIRIT
Do you feel controlled? Learn more about what the Bible says about this manipulating principality's influence.

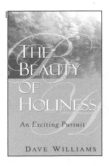

DEVELOPING THE SPIRIT OF A CONQUEROR
Take back what the enemy has stolen from you. Learn how to engage your authority and Develop the Spirit of a Conqueror.

BEAUTY OF HOLINESS
We face the choice — holiness or rebellion. True holiness comes about by working together in cooperation with the Holy Spirit.

ABCs OF SUCCESS & HAPPINESS
God wants to give you every good gift, so it's time to accept the responsibility for your success today!

These and other books available from Dave Williams and:

DECAPOLIS PUBLISHING

FOR YOUR SPIRITUAL GROWTH

Here's the help you need for your spiritual journey. These books will encourage you, and give you guidance as you seek to draw close to Jesus and learn of Him. Prepare yourself for fantastic growth!

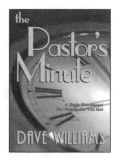

QUESTIONS I HAVE ANSWERED
Get answers to many of the questions you've always wanted to ask a pastor!

THE PASTOR'S MINUTE
A daily devotional for people on the go! Powerful topics will help you grow even when you're in a hurry.

ANGELS: THEY ARE WATCHING YOU!
The Bible tells more than you might think about these powerful beings.

THE WORLD BEYOND
What will Heaven be like? What happens there? Will we see relatives who have gone before us? Who REALLY goes to Heaven?

FILLED!
Learn how you can be filled with the mightiest power in the universe. Find out what could be missing from your life.

STRATEGIC GLOBAL MISSION
Read touching stories about God's plan for accelerating the Gospel globally through reaching children and training pastors.

These and other books available from Dave Williams and:

DECAPOLIS PUBLISHING

FOR YOUR SPIRITUAL GROWTH

Here's the help you need for your spiritual journey. These books will encourage you, and give you guidance as you seek to draw close to Jesus and learn of Him. Prepare yourself for fantastic growth!

HOW TO BE A HIGH PERFORMANCE BELIEVER
Pour in the nine spiritual additives for real power in your Christian life.

SECRET OF POWER WITH GOD
Tap into the real power with God; the power of prayer. It will change your life!

THE NEW LIFE . . .
You can get off to a great start on your exciting life with Jesus! Prepare for something wonderful.

MIRACLE RESULTS OF FASTING
You can receive MIRACLE benefits, spiritually and physically, with this practical Christian discipline.

WHAT TO DO IF YOU MISS THE RAPTURE
If you miss the Rapture, there may still be hope, but you need to follow these clear survival tactics.

THE AIDS PLAGUE
Is there hope? Yes, but only Jesus can bring a total and lasting cure to AIDS.

These and other books available from Dave Williams and:

FOR YOUR SPIRITUAL GROWTH

Here's the help you need for your spiritual journey. These books will encourage you, and give you guidance as you seek to draw close to Jesus and learn of Him. Prepare yourself for fantastic growth!

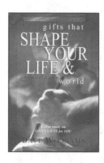

THE ART OF PACESETTING LEADERSHIP
You can become a successful leader with this proven leadership development course.

GIFTS THAT SHAPE YOUR LIFE
Learn which ministry best fits you, and discover your God-given personality gifts, as well as the gifts of others.

GROWING UP IN OUR FATHER'S FAMILY
You can have a family relationship with your heavenly father. Learn how God cares for you.

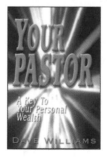

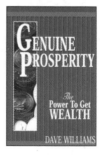

SUPERNATURAL SOULWINNING
How will we reach our family, friends, and neighbors in this short time before Christ's return?

YOUR PASTOR: A KEY TO YOUR PERSONAL WEALTH
By honoring your pastor you can actually be setting yourself up for a financial blessing from God!

GENUINE PROSPERITY
Learn what it means to be truly prosperous! God gives us the power to get wealth!

FOR YOUR SPIRITUAL GROWTH

Here's the help you need for your spiritual journey. These books will encourage you, and give you guidance as you seek to draw close to Jesus and learn of Him. Prepare yourself for fantastic growth!

SOMEBODY OUT THERE NEEDS YOU
Along with the gift of salvation comes the great privilege of spreading the Gospel of Jesus Christ.

SEVEN SIGNPOSTS ON THE ROAD TO SPIRITUAL MATURITY
Examine your life to see where you are on the road to spiritual maturity.

THE PASTOR'S PAY
How much is your pastor worth? Who should set his pay? Discover the scriptural guidelines for paying your pastor.

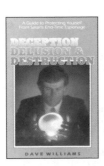

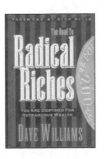

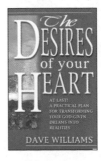

DECEPTION, DELUSION & DESTRUCTION
Recognize spiritual deception and unmask spiritual blindness.

THE ROAD TO RADICAL RICHES
Are you ready to jump from "barely getting by" to God's plan for putting you on the road to Radical Riches?

THE DESIRES OF YOUR HEART
Yes, Jesus wants to give you the desires of your heart, and make them realities.

These and other books available from Dave Williams and:

DECAPOLIS PUBLISHING

FOR YOUR SUCCESSFUL LIFE

These video cassettes will give you successful principles to apply to your whole life. Each a different topic, and each a fantastic teaching of how living by God's Word can give you total success!

THE PRESENCE OF GOD
Find out how you can have a more dynamic relationship with the Holy Spirit.

FILLED WITH THE HOLY SPIRIT
You can rejoice and share with others in this wonderful experience of God.

GIFTS THAT CHANGE YOUR WORLD
Learn which ministry best fits you, and discover your God-given personality gifts, as well as the gifts of others.

THE SCHOOL OF PACESET-TING LEADERSHIP
Leaders are made, not born. You can become a successful leader with this proven leadership development course.

MIRACLE RESULTS OF FASTING
Fasting is your secret weapon in spiritual warfare. Learn how you'll benefit spiritually and physically! Six video messages.

A SPECIAL LADY
If you feel used and abused, this video will show you how you really are in the eyes of Jesus. You are special!

These and other videos available from Dave Williams and:

DECAPOLIS PUBLISHING

FOR YOUR SUCCESSFUL LIFE

These video cassettes will give you successful principles to apply to your whole life. Each a different topic, and each a fantastic teaching of how living by God's Word can give you total success!

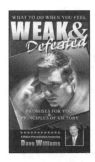

HOW TO BE A HIGH PERFORMANCE BELIEVER
Pour in the nine spiritual additives for real power in your Christian life.

THE UGLY WORMS OF JUDGMENT
Recognizing the decay of judgment in your life is your first step back into God's fullness.

WHAT TO DO WHEN YOU FEEL WEAK AND DEFEATED
Learn about God's plan to bring you out of defeat and into His principles of victory!

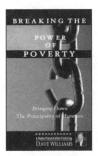

WHY SOME ARE NOT HEALED
Discover the obstacles that hold people back from receiving their miracle and how God can help them receive the very best!

BREAKING THE POWER OF POVERTY
The principality of mammon will try to keep you in poverty. Put God FIRST and watch Him bring you into a wealthy place.

HERBS FOR HEALTH
A look at the concerns and fears of modern medicine. Learn the correct ways to open the doors to your healing.

These and other videos available from Dave Williams and:

DECAPOLIS PUBLISHING

RUNNING YOUR RACE

These simple but powerful audio cassette singles will help give you the edge you need. Run your race to win!

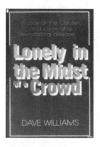

LONELY IN THE MIDST OF A CROWD
Loneliness is a devastating disease. Learn how to trust and count on others to help.

HERBS FOR HEALTH
A look at the concerns and fears of modern medicine. Learn the correct ways to open the doors to your healing.

HOW TO GET ANYTHING YOU WANT
You can learn the way to get anything you want from God!

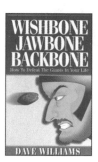

WISHBONE, JAWBONE, BACKBONE
Learn about King David, and how his three "bones" for success can help you in your life quest.

FATAL ENTICEMENTS
Learn how you can avoid the vice-like grip of sin and it's fatal enticements that hold people captive.

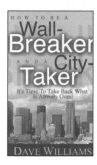

HOW TO BE A WALL BREAKER AND A CITY TAKER
You can be a powerful force for advancing the Kingdom of Jesus Christ!

These and other audio tapes available from Dave Williams and:

DECAPOLIS PUBLISHING

EXPANDING YOUR FAITH

These exciting audio teaching series will help you to grow
and mature in your walk with Christ. Get ready for amazing
new adventures in faith!

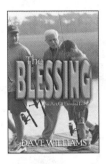  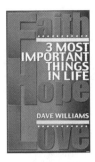

THE BLESSING
Explore the many ways that God can use you to bless others, and how He can correct the missed blessing.

SIN'S GRIP
Learn how you can avoid the vice-like grip of sin and its fatal enticements that hold people captive.

FAITH, HOPE, & LOVE
Listen and let these three "most important things in life" change you.

  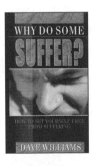

**PSALM 91
THE PROMISE OF
PROTECTION**
Everyone is looking for protection in these perilous times. God promises protection for those who rest in Him.

**DEVELOPING
THE SPIRIT OF A
CONQUEROR**
You can be a conqueror through Christ! Also, find out how to keep those things that you have conquered.

WHY DO SOME SUFFER
Find out why some people seem to have suffering in their lives, and how to avoid it in your life.

*These and other audio tapes
available from Dave Williams and:*

EXPANDING YOUR FAITH

These exciting audio teaching series will help you to grow and mature in your walk with Christ. Get ready for amazing new adventures in faith!

ABCs OF SUCCESS AND HAPPINESS
Learn how to go after God's promises for your life. Happiness and success can be yours today!

FORGIVENESS
The miracle remedy for many of life's problems is found in this basic key for living.

UNTANGLING YOUR TROUBLES
You can be a "trouble untangler" with the help of Jesus!

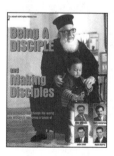

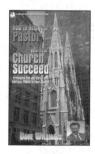

HOW TO BE A HIGH PERFORMANCE BELIEVER
Put in the nine spiritual additives to help run your race and get the prize!

BEING A DISCIPLE AND MAKING DISCIPLES
You can learn to be a "disciple maker" to almost anyone.

HOW TO HELP YOUR PASTOR & CHURCH SUCCEED
You can be an integral part of your church's & pastor's success.

These and other audio tapes available from Dave Williams and:

DECAPOLIS PUBLISHING